Enthusiastic Comments from Readers of Our Books

The following are just a few of the comments from more than seven hundred letters and emails that we have received pertaining to our publications. For additional comments, see our website: lamplight.net.

Trust God for Your Finances

There are more than 150,000 copies of *Trust God for Your Finances* in print. This book has been translated into seven foreign languages.

- "I have translated *Trust God for Your Finances* into Thai. I intended to make about 50 or 60 photocopies of this translation to distribute among friends. My pastor asked for 700 copies to distribute at the special yearly conference for pastors. My immediate thought was that I could not do this, but he urged me to pray and try my best. Surprisingly, it worked out. Thank God. More than 1,000 people attended the conference. Seven hundred copies were distributed to only the pastors, elders and deacons who really wanted the book. After the conference, we had so many calls that another 2,000 copies were printed. Thank you, Mr. Hartman, for this book which is helping so many Thai Christians." (Thailand)

- "I bought your book, *Trust God for Your Finances,* at a church I was attending in Virginia in the 1980s. This book transformed my life. It was all Bible-based and solid in every way. I married a Bulgarian pastor who started the church here during

Communism and the underground church. We have pastored together for 22 years. I gave your book to my husband and he consumed it. He kept it near his Bible all the time. God has raised him up to be influential in this nation. He has written a book titled *The Covenant of Provision* dealing with finances. Your book helped him so much to form his ideas about the rightful use of money. This book has influenced my husband more than almost any other book. It was so timely and needed coming out of a Communist society. Thank you so much for this book." (Bulgaria)

- "Today we had a ministry partner join us for lunch. He said that the book, *Trust God for Your Finances*, that we had translated into Hebrew was the most powerful book he had ever read on the subject. I shared with him the wonderful story of how you shared the book with us and how many Israelis have been enlightened in that area as a result of reading the book. You both are a blessing and a treasure in God's kingdom." (Israel)

What Does God Say?
- "Your book *What Does God Say?* is one of the greatest books I have ever read. You tell the truth and back it up with Scripture. I started crime very young. I have spent a large portion of my life behind bars. I have so much to be ashamed of and things that I am very sorry for. I have almost wasted my life. I say almost because this book caused me to realize that God loves even me no matter what I have done. In your book I read that there is no condemnation in Christ Jesus. Do you have any idea what it means to feel no condemnation when society says to lock me up because I am guilty? My sins and all the crimes I have committed have been washed away. I cannot explain how it feels to know that someone is really proud of me. That someone is Jesus. I am taking this book home with me. Even though I don't have much education, I can understand it very well. I now know that I am saved and I am forgiven. Thank you very much for writing this book." (Florida)

- "Several months ago, you sent me a copy of your book titled *What Does God Say?*. This book is amazing. First of all, I could understand it. My English is not great. I have been a Muslim all my life. I was taught as a child what I was supposed to believe. When I was searching for real truth, I met the Master and received Jesus Christ as my Savior. When I read your book, it filled so much of the void and loneliness that I was filled with. I will be sharing Jesus and *What Does God Say?* with my family and with other Muslims. Please pray for me as I may not be welcomed in my own home town for finding this wonderful Jesus." (Ghana)

- "I am a sixty-two year old retired official in the Royal Thai government. I am a born-again Christian. Throughout my life I think I am a good Christian by going to church. Recently a friend of mine gave me a book titled *What Does God Say?*. At first I thought what could God say to someone like me who prides himself on being a faithful church-goer? When I started reading, however, it was like being awakened from a long sleep. Never before did I know God the way I feel now. I feel so ashamed of being so ignorant all these years thinking that just going to church is enough to be called a good Christian. I don't know how to thank the authors of this book who opened my heart and mind to see God the true way that He is. The remaining years of my life will not be the same with this newfound knowledge of our Savior. Better late than never." (Thailand)

Quiet Confidence in the Lord
- "As soon as I was diagnosed with prostate cancer, I began to meditate on the Scripture and your explanation of the Scripture in *Quiet Confidence in the Lord*. I carried this book with me everywhere for several weeks. The specialist at the Lahey Clinic in Boston told me I was the calmest person with this diagnosis that he had ever seen. During the pre-op and the surgery, a number of people commented on how calm I was. I experienced a lot of discomfort during the difficult first week at home after the surgery. I focused constantly on the Scripture in this wonderful book. I was remarkably calm. Thank you for writing this book that has helped me so much." (Massachusetts)

- "After I graduated from Bible school, I went outside of my country for mission work with my wife. After we were there for nine months, my wife died suddenly. My sorrow was great. I read your book titled *Quiet Confidence in the Lord*. This book spoke to my heart. All twenty-three chapters were written for me. God changed me through this book and comforted me and took away my sorrow. Through the blood of Jesus I entered God's rest. I can give a great recommendation for this book to anyone who is filled with sorrow and grief. I pray that many people will read this book and develop quiet confidence in the Lord as I did. Thank you so much for sending this book to me. May God bless you and your ministry." (Ethiopia)

- "*Quiet Confidence in the Lord* is with me at work each day. I have read and underlined passages that lift my heart and help me to understand something I've known all along and that is that I am not alone and that God cares very much that I'm in the midst of great adversity. I asked God to send me a comforter, someone who would put their arms around me and say, 'I understand and I care.' The answer to that prayer is in you and Judy. Thanks to *Quiet Confidence of the Lord* I am, for the first time in my life, learning to focus on God and not my problems. Thank you both for your ministry. Your books are a tremendous blessing to hurting people all over the world." (Washington, DC)

Receive Healing from the Lord

- "Your great book, *Receive Healing from the Lord*, has amazed me. This book has been my daily bread. I have followed all of God's instructions in your book. My children and my wife were healed from severe illness. I was sick myself just before an important crusade. I meditated on the Scripture in your book for the entire night. I was totally healed. The following day God did wonders as He healed many people. Since then, people have been coming to receive their healing at our home and church almost every day. Many healings are taking place at our services. This book is wonderful. I am abundantly blessed by it." (Zambia)

- "My husband and I served in the mission field in Swaziland, Africa, for three and a half years. Upon our arrival, Lamplight Ministries sent us four mailbags full of Jack and Judy's books. Because Swaziland is so laden with HIV/AIDS, we were able to use the book, *Receive Healing from the Lord,* with the people in Swaziland to see many people come to a saving knowledge of the Lord Jesus Christ and His perfect will regarding healing. We saw mothers with very sick children who themselves also were afflicted with AIDS respond to the many Scriptures that are part of the book, actually believing that it was meant for them. Had it not been for the use of this book and the other books you sent, we would not have had such success in teaching a Bible study about the truth in God's Word to these people. We gave out your books and told the people that the book was theirs to keep. We saw such joy and surprise on the faces of these impoverished people. We appreciate the ongoing generosity of Lamplight Ministries for 'such a time as this' in these days where there is so much need and want. We will forever be thankful that we can count on the Word of God through the books written by Jack and Judy as effective tools in the transformation of people's lives." (Swaziland)

- "Thank you very much for sending me your book, *Receive Healing from the Lord.* After reading the first chapter I realized that this book could be the solution for my wife's failing health. We decided to read the book together every day. My wife was healed and restored after carefully following the scriptural principles that you explained. We are humbled by how we had struggled and panicked trying to find an answer. God gave us the solution in your book. We are so grateful to you. We love you and we are praying for you." (Zambia)

Effective Prayer
- "I thank God for your book titled *Effective Prayer.* This book came to me at the right time. Since reading this book, God has done great wonders in my life and ministry. Our whole church is being affected by what we have learned about the power of prayer. I have read many books on prayer, but this

one is unique. I no longer pray amiss. My prayer life has become much more effective. Your book has helped me to persevere in prayer much longer than before. This is a great book. I love it. I treasure this book. I do not know how to thank you. I pray that God will bless you both with long life and that you will enjoy the fruit of your labour." (Zambia)

- "Your book *Effective Prayer* is a great blessing to me. After reading this book I have so much more understanding about prayer. It is very easy to learn from all that you are teaching and all of the Scriptures in it. I now understand much more about the significance of prayer in my daily life, why I should pray and how to pray. You have enlightened my mind. I know that my loving Father wants me to pray all the time. I have learned to pray God's answer instead of focusing on the problem. This book is very vital to my daily life. I am so thankful to both of you for another great book for people who need answers. Thank you so much for the great understanding that I found in this book." (the Philippines)

- "I have been studying your book *Effective Prayer.* This book has inspired me to do a lot more praying. Praying to God is such a privilege. To know that God is just waiting for me to come and talk with Him is tremendous. The way you brought out the gift of being baptized in the Holy Spirit and praying in tongues will make it easier for people to receive this much-needed gift in their lives. Our pastor is using your book to teach on prayer. I have given copies of this book to many people in our church. I gave one to another pastor in our town. I love you both in the Lord Jesus Christ. I thank God for you and for allowing Him to continue to use you in the body of Christ." (Oklahoma)

What Will Heaven Be Like?

- "On the very first page of your book on heaven I was spellbound. The material read so quickly and coherently that it was like having a conversation with a Christian friend. I could really feel the excitement as we talked about the throne of God and its radiance. Those who are curious about heaven will be so delighted and joyful when they read this book. I think the questions at the end of the book are a great idea. This book is a ready-made classroom treasure. I was deeply moved by the gentle loving approach and the manner this material was presented to me, the reader. I can hardly wait to read your other books. You have gained a new fan and admirer of your special way of presenting the kingdom of heaven and God's love for us." (Mississippi)

- "I came to China from Cambodia where I was a captain in the army. I was a Buddhist. Four weeks before I came to China, I had a dream where Jesus appeared to me. When I woke up the following morning, I looked for Christians to explain more about Jesus Christ to me. After I came to China, I met a Christian man who gave me the book *What Will Heaven Be Like?*. This book answered many questions for me. My English is not very good, but this book is written in very simple English. I have found new life through this book. Please pray for me so that I can share Jesus with my parents and my Buddhist friends when I go back to Cambodia." (China)

- "I am the Youth Director of our church and I'm leading a group of high school students in a Bible study of your book on heaven. We all respect your opinions and have found your book to be an excellent springboard for discussion. It is thought-provoking and informative. This book has much substance and is well organized." (California)

Never, Never Give Up
- "I am a 68-year-old businessman. At my age I should be enjoying a life way past retirement. It is not so. In 1997 Thailand suffered a severe economic crunch and my business almost went down under. It took me many years to try to come back. Just as I thought I was climbing out of the black hole, another crisis hit two years ago. This time I am too old to fight, but I have no choice but to go on. I thought that God and I were very close. However, after the first crisis hit I sort of lost my faith along with my hope. After the second crisis hit, I thought that God had forsaken me. I all but lost my faith totally until one day a good friend gave me a book, *Never, Never Give Up*. At first I didn't want to read it. However,

insisted by my friend, I did. I stayed up the whole night finishing the book. By morning I kneeled down and begged God to forgive me for my foolishness. I felt so ashamed for my behavior. I begged Him to accept me back. After I did that, I know that God has forgiven me. Now I am back to feeling close to Him again. I am so happy and grateful for this book. God is great!" (Thailand)

- "Thanks for being there when you are so much needed by all of us. After seven major operations I am beginning to walk again and help others which is the full purpose of my existence which Jesus Christ has set before me. Your book, *Never, Never Give Up*, stayed by my pillow along with my Bible while I was recuperating from these operations. When I re-read it, I was charged with peace and energy again. The pain diminishes and I can speak of God's infinite love and mercy to others who are facing similar trials. Thank you for writing this God-inspired book." (Florida)

- "Suicide has shown its face in my mind. I found myself falling deeper and deeper into the pit of hell. My life seemed so grim. I could not see where I could make a difference and was planning to believe that if I chose to leave this life it would not matter. When I received *Never, Never Give Up* I read the first three chapters that evening. When I arrived at page ninety, your verse changed my life. I want you to know that I have been delivered from this season of trial. I rededicated my life to the Lord and feel wonderful. Thank you so much for your work. Through our Lord you have saved my life. Thank you for my life back." (Texas)

Overcoming Fear
- "Thank you for sending your books to the Philippines. I was very blessed to read *Overcoming Fear*. This book explained the sources of fear and what I should do to overcome fear. It is really a blessing to know all of this information that helped me to overcome the fear I have felt all these years. I have cherished every chapter in the book. It has become food for my soul. Thank you so much for explaining all of this so well. I have learned that I should never be afraid of anyone because

I can be absolutely certain that God lives in my heart. This is great assurance because I know that God is greater than anything I will ever face in this life. This book has been a great blessing in my life. God bless you both." (the Philippines)

- "I want to thank you immediately for your new book, *Overcoming Fear*. I have read every one of your books and given copies to many people, but I want to tell you that I believe this is your best book ever. I can hardly put it down. The day I received it I stayed up late, even though I was very tired, to read the first four chapters. The next morning I read two more chapters before going to work. This book is very inspiring. It gives me great peace. God's peace is so great that I cannot describe it. I have almost finished reading this book. When I am done, I will immediately read it again. Enclosed is a check for ten copies of this book plus a contribution to Lamplight Ministries. Thank you, Jack and Judy, for writing this wonderful book." (Massachusetts)

- "I want to thank you for publishing the book *Overcoming Fear*. I am reading mine for the second time. I cannot tell you how comforting it is. The way you have put information along with the right Bible verses is so truly helpful. As world conditions worsen, I can tell you that this book will be a constant companion alongside my Bible. I am so grateful for you both. Keep up the good work. You are making a big difference in peoples' lives. You have in mine." (Minnesota)

Victory Over Adversity

- "I am a pure and proud Dutchman married to a Tanzanian woman. I have had a lot of problems staying with an African wife in Europe. I love my wife so much, but the environment for my wife was not good enough in terms of getting a job. This affected us very much to the extent that I was even planning to relocate to Tanzania for the sake of my wife and childrens' future. Thank God that an angel was sent to me by the name of Jim who gave me a book, *Victory over Adversity*. This book is amazing and great. It contains the answers to my problems and is a great encouragement to me. As a Dutchman I find it very interesting to read a book with simple English.

Putting the facts of this book into practice has changed my life greatly. I have found a new job. My wife has found a good job. The thoughts of relocating to Tanzania have faded. My faith has increased and my commitment to God has grown. I pray that God will bless the writers of this book and also the man who gave me this book. My wife and I are always reading this book. It is our source of strength." (Holland)

- "I praise God for His living Word. Thank you for the books that you have sent to China. You cannot imagine what *Victory over Adversity* did in my life as a young believer. Not only is the language clear and accessible, but the content is very rewarding. I learned a lot from this book. I now meditate day and night on the Word of God. I am in the presence of God often. I am confident that I can overcome any adversity in the precious name of Jesus Christ. May God bless you and fill you with His infinite grace, Mr. Jack and his wife." (China)

- "I am a 22-year-old college student in Thailand. My family is half Christian. My mother is a Christian whereas my father is a Buddhist. I am the eldest daughter of my parents with one younger brother and sister. All three of us have been baptized as Christians since birth. Frankly, I have never had much faith in God and always have had problems with both of my parents. I think that they don't understand me. They think I don't listen to them. Last month my mother was given a book, *Victory over Adversity,* by her friend. Out of curiosity I took the book and read it before she did. I could not put it down. For the first time I felt that God is real and is close to me. I cried and cried and felt sorry for my past behavior toward God and my parents. I went to my mother and apologized, to her great surprise. Now I go to church with her every Sunday. I am very thankful to my mother's friend who gave her this book and also to the writers of this book who have changed my life and brought me to God which my mother could not do. Thank you both!" (Thailand)

Exchange Your Worries for God's Perfect Peace

- "*Exchange Your Worries for God's Perfect Peace* is a masterpiece. I am reading this book to the people here in the

Philippines. I saw tears flowing down their faces as I read them parts of this book. I must get this book translated into their language. I am reading this book for the second time. After 30 years in the ministry I have finally learned how to turn my worries over to God. I have learned more from this book in the last few months than I have ever learned in my life. I will not allow my copy of this book to leave my presence. I thank God for you." (the Philippines)

- "I just want to tell you how much I appreciate you and your excellent book, *Exchange Your Worries for God's Perfect Peace*. I have read all of your books several times each. I continually go back to refer to the notes I have made in your books. I have done this for close to 15 years and pages are falling out of your books. I read the Bible daily. Your books are a close second to the Bible. I have never found another Christian author who teaches me more about God's Word and speaks directly to my heart as your writings do. Thank you for helping me appreciate and respect the Word of God." (Wisconsin)

- "I was in despair struggling with my life and ministry. *Exchange Your Worries for God's Perfect Peace* has strengthened me and encouraged my heart. My country is often threatened by disasters. Your book and the Scripture in it has helped me to focus on God, no matter what circumstances I have experienced and will face in the future. The language in the book is very clear and easy to understand for someone like me who uses English as a second language. I have been blessed by reading this book. My faith in Jesus has increased. Thank you for sending this book to me. I thank God that I know you. You are a blessing." (Indonesia)

God's Joy Regardless of Circumstances

- "*God's Joy Regardless of Circumstances* came to me right on time. Being in prison for 20 years for a crime I didn't commit and then having to deal with severe family problems is not a morsel that is easy to swallow. My oldest daughter was pregnant and we were looking forward to having my first grandson born. We were very pained to learn that my daughter had to lose her baby. In the midst of dealing with this problem, you sent me a free copy of *God's Joy Regardless of Circumstances.* When I avidly started to read this book, my daughter underwent surgery, lost her baby and faced uncertainty and despair. *God's Joy Regardless of Circumstances* pulled us through. Thank you also for sending a free copy of this book to my daughter. May God continue blessing Lamplight Ministries." (Florida)

- "Many thanks for sending me *God's Joy Regardless of Circumstances.* This book has been a real stream in the desert that I have been able to drink from. I have been blessed tremendously by this book. My life has not been the same since I started reading it. I have used this book to help many people on my radio programme every Sunday. Many people have given their lives to Christ because of these messages." (Zambia)

- "Only this year I faced a lot of challenges. As a result I became bitter at heart. The wonderful Scripture verses in *God's Joy Regardless of Circumstances* took away my bitterness. I am happy now. This book has instructed me how to handle any situation with God's joy. I now can see God's solution to my life challenges by the presence of God's joy inside me. Your God-given insight has given new meaning to my spiritual life. Thank you for the encouragement through your writings." (Lome-Togo West Africa)

God's Wisdom Is Available to You

- "I did not sleep last night after reading your book *God's Wisdom is Available to You.* Thank you for your wonderful work. Because of persecution against my ministry, I spent a considerable amount of time in the hospital because of depression. I am now well and healthy in Jesus' name. Thank you for your help. I will be teaching members of my church from key text in your book. Please be my mentor, teacher and counselor." (Ghana)

- "I thank God each and every day for Jack and Judy Hartman. When I started reading your book on wisdom, everything was going wrong in my life. This book revived my spirit and my faith in God. It has changed my life. The Bible used to be like Greek to me. Now I can read it and understand it. I can't put this book down because I know I need to absorb it. I'm going through it for a second time. This book is one of the best things that has ever happened to me. I thank you both and I thank God." (Florida)

- "You did a fantastic job on this book. It is an encyclopedia on God's wisdom. The writing style is just great. Many books don't bring the reader through the subject the way this book does. I'm very impressed with that. You have made it a real joy for me to study and re-digest Scripture. This book has been very good for me." (North Carolina)

A Close and Intimate Relationship with God

- "Your book, *A Close and Intimate Relationship with God,* is tremendous. I thought that I had a close relationship with God, but this book really opened my eyes. I now can see many things that I still need to do to be even closer to God. I couldn't put this book down. When I had to stop reading, I couldn't wait to get back to it the next day. Every chapter is filled with Scripture that is very helpful to me. I will be making many changes in my life as a result of reading this awesome book. Thank you and God bless you." (New Hampshire)

- "Thank you for giving me a copy of your book *A Close and Intimate Relationship with God.* This book is written so clearly that all instructions are to the point. My life has been greatly changed and refreshed. The presence of God has become very strong in my life. I am at peace trusting my God to meet every need. My mind is totally on God. I can clearly hear His voice. I am receiving guidance and direction from Him as a result of this book. I cannot afford to spend a day without reading this book. I carry it with me wherever I go." (Zambia)

- "Thank you for your book titled *A Close and Intimate Relationship with God.* This inspiring book helped me to draw closer to our heavenly Father. In Chapter 25 you said that Paul and Silas were praising God in prison. I was having a challenging day when I read this chapter. God spoke through your book to praise Him no matter what circumstances I faced.

Thank you for that inspiration. The information on dying to self in the last chapter where Paul said that he dies daily really encouraged me. I am learning to do much better putting God first, others second and myself last. Thank you at Lamplight Ministries for the thousands of people around the world that you are supporting. May the dear Lord bless you abundantly." (China)

Unshakable Faith in Almighty God

- "I thank God for the book *Unshakable Faith in Almighty God*. Because I am not indigenous Chinese, it is not easy to fellowship with the local Chinese. When I got this book I was able to see a way in the wilderness. It became my guide and light every day. When I was just about to give up Christianity, God at the right time provided this book to me. The truths and clear instruction in this book are direct from the throne of God. I am determined to move on with God come what may. I praise God that is He able to raise people we have never seen like Jack and Judy Hartman to speak into our lives through their publications. God bless the Hartman family. One day when Christ comes it will be exciting for them to see how they have influenced the world for God in Jesus' name. I am so grateful for these free books that cost a lot of money in publishing, printing and postage." (China)

- "I have been pastoring in Belgium for the past 15 years. In the past our church was flourishing and doing very well until late last year when my praise and worship leader decided to break away and form another church. This was a very big blow to us as a church. Most of our strong and committed members left the church with some of the church instruments. My wife almost gave up. She was discouraged. This also affected our finances. Pastor Jim gave me a book titled *Unshakable Faith in Almighty God*. Before I read this book my faith was shaken and I almost gave up. This book took me step by step to show me how to make my faith grow. You cannot read this book and remain the same. I have been using the book to preach to the few members that remain with us. In the past four months we have experienced revival. The anointing is so strong and the members have been strengthened so much through the preaching from this book. We are determined to not give up. God bless the Hartmans for being a blessing to us in Europe." (Belgium)

- "*Unshakable Faith in Almighty God* has amazed me. The language is so simple and very clear to understand. This book is powerful and life-changing. I will always hang on to this book. Brother Hartman, God's favour and wisdom are so great on your life. I believe this book is written on very heavy anointing from God. Your reward in heaven will be so great. All those who have sown seeds in your ministry should rejoice. When I wake up, I read this book. Before going to bed, I read it. I will continue to go through it again and again. Your ministry is a big blessing to me. You are always in our prayers." (Zambia)

How to Study the Bible

- "Your book, *How to Study the Bible*, is a gem. Since I became a Christian 41 years ago, I have studied the Bible using a variety of methods. Your method is simple and straightforward. It involves hard work, but the rewards are real. I have read several of your books and this book is the one I would highly recommend to any Christian because this book is the foundation. God bless you, brother." (England)

- "My wife and I are utilizing the Bible study method that you explained in *How to Study the Bible*. We are really growing spiritually as a result. Our old methods of study were not nearly as fruitful. Thank you for writing about your method." (Idaho)

- "I have read almost all of your books and they are outstanding. The one that blessed me the most was *How to Study the Bible*. The study part was excellent, but the meditation chapters were very, very beneficial. I am indebted to you for sharing these. I purchased 30 copies to give to friends. Every earnest student of God's Word needs a copy." (Tennessee)

Increased Energy and Vitality

- "It is so great to meet Christians on the same wave length. In your book *Increased Energy and Vitality*, you are writing almost word for word in some cases what I have been saying to patients for almost 30 years." (Ohio)

- "Last year I obtained a copy of your book *Increased Energy and Vitality*. My wife and I have read and have in fact changed our ways of eating and drinking and exercising because of your influence. We thoroughly appreciate this God-centered message that is so well presented. I have enclosed an order for more of these books. We know many people we wish to help. This is the first step in spreading the news you have so generously put together. Thank you for your efforts. May God continue your leadership in writing, speaking and guidance." (Illinois)

- "I have benefited tremendously from reading and personally applying the principles learned from your book *Increased Energy and Vitality*. By applying your methods, I have gained additional energy especially during my low periods from 2:00 p.m. to 4:00 p.m. I highly recommend your book to others. Keep up the good work." (Florida)

100 Years from Today

- "*100 Years From Today* told me that going to church and doing good deeds won't get me to heaven. I believe in Jesus Christ. I believe He died for our sins and that He forgives us for what we did wrong. Heaven is where I belong. I am born again. I have a new life. This book has changed my life." (Florida)

- "I am writing to express my deep and profound appreciation for your book *100 Years from Today*. I recently began attending a Bible-based church where I found a copy of this book in their lending library. I read the book in one sitting, reading the words aloud to myself. Your book explained details from the Bible that I had not learned before. I thank you for taking the time and effort to write this book. My written words can never fully express how grateful I am to you. By my actions, a changed life and a deep sense of peace, I hope to bear fruit by helping others." (Massachusetts)

- "I find it hard to put *100 Years from Today* down. I read the whole book in a day and a half. I never knew how much pain and suffering Jesus went through to pay for my sins. I learned how much He loves us." (Florida)

Nuggets of Faith
- "Your books, tapes and meditation cards are really a blessing to me. They came at just the right time. I am preparing sermons on faith from *Nuggets of Faith*. I want the congregation to be constantly learning God's Word in order to have much more faith. I also have been encouraged personally through that book. It is awesome. Thank you for your powerful and inspiring publications." (Zambia)
- "We give *Nuggets of Faith* to people who are hospitalized, for birthdays, to saved and unsaved. Everyone who has received one tells us 'It's the best little book I've ever read. It's so clear and easy to understand.'" (Indiana)
- "I work as a store manager. Today I was told that I was no longer needed. Praise Jesus that only two months prior to this date I had accepted the Lord Jesus as my personal Lord and Savior. I have faith that the Lord was working to bring me to a new direction. I am writing to thank you for your excellent book *Nuggets of Faith*. The moment I arrived home after having been dismissed, I received this book in the mail. I completed this short but awesome book in a little over two hours. It has helped my faith to grow stronger and I know that I will begin a great new journey tomorrow. God bless you." (New York)

Comments on our Scripture Meditation Cards

- "My back was hurting so badly that I couldn't get comfortable. I was miserable whether I sat or stood or laid down. I didn't know what to do. Suddenly I thought of the Scripture cards on healing that my husband had purchased. I decided to meditate on the Scripture in these cards. I was only on the second card when, all of a sudden, I felt heat go from my neck down through my body. The Lord had healed me. I never knew it could happen so fast. The pain has not come back." (Idaho)

- "My wife and I use your Scripture cards every day when we pray. I read the card for that day in English and then my wife repeats it in Norwegian. We then pray based upon the Scripture reference on that day's card. These cards have been very beneficial to us. We would like to see the Scripture cards published in the Norwegian language." (Norway)

- "Your Scripture cards have been very helpful to my wife and myself. We have taped them to the walls in our home and we meditate on them constantly. I also take four or five cards with me every day when I go to work. I meditate on them while I drive. The Scripture on these cards is a constant source of encouragement to us. We ask for permission to translate *Trust God for Your Finances*. This book is badly needed by the people in Turkey." (This permission was granted.) (Turkey)

- "My mom is 95 years old. She was in the Bergen-Belsen Concentration Camp in Germany from 1943 to 1945. She has always had a lot of worry and fear. My mother was helped greatly in overcoming this problem by your Scripture cards titled *Freedom from Worry and Fear*. She was helped so much that she asked me to order another set to give to a friend." (California)

- "I am overwhelmed about the revelations in your Scripture Meditation Cards. These Scripture cards have helped me so much that I cannot write enough on this sheet of paper. We have gone through a five-day programme in our church using the Scripture cards. My faith has increased tremendously. I no longer am submitting to my own will and desires, but I am now submitting to the will of God and it is so fantastic. God bless you, Jack and Judy Hartman." (Ghana)

- "I am very enthusiastic about your Scripture cards and your tape titled *Receive Healing from the Lord*. I love your tape. The clarity of your voice and your sincerity and compassion will encourage sick people. They can listen to this tape throughout the day, before they go to sleep at night, while they are driving to the doctor's office, in the hospital, etc. The tape is filled with Scripture and many good comments on Scripture. This cassette tape and your Scripture cards on healing are powerful tools that will help many sick people." (Tennessee) (NOTE: The ten cassette tapes for our Scripture Meditation Cards are available on 60 minute CDs as well.)

- "I meditate constantly on the healing cards and listen to your tape on healing over and over. Your voice is so soothing. You are a wonderful teacher. My faith is increasing constantly." (New Hampshire).

- "I thank God for you. I carry your Scripture Meditation Cards in my purse. The Scriptures you have chosen are all powerful. What a blessing to be able to meditate on the Word of God at any time, anywhere. Thank you for your hard work. The Scripture cards are a blessing to me." (Canada)

Books written by Jack Hartman
Trust God for Your Finances
What Will Heaven Be Like?
Never, Never Give Up
How to Study the Bible
Quiet Confidence in the Lord
One Hundred Years from Today
Nuggets of Faith
God's Will for Your Life

Books co-authored by Jack and Judy Hartman
God's Instructions for Growing Older
Effective Prayer
Overcoming Fear
A Close and Intimate Relationship with God
God's Joy Regardless of Circumstances
Victory Over Adversity
What Does God Say?
Receive Healing from the Lord
Unshakable Faith in Almighty God
Exchange Your Worries for God's Perfect Peace
God's Wisdom Is Available to You
Increased Energy and Vitality

Scripture Meditation Cards
co-authored by Jack and Judy Hartman
Receive Healing from the Lord
Freedom from Worry and Fear
Enjoy God's Wonderful Peace
God Is Always with You
Continually Increasing Faith in God
Receive God's Blessings in Adversity
Financial Instructions from God
Find God's Will for Your Life
A Closer Relationship with the Lord
Our Father's Wonderful Love

God's Instructions for Growing Older

Jack and Judy Hartman

Lamplight Ministries, Inc.

Dunedin, Florida

We invite you to visit our website: www.lamplight.net. You also can see all of our other Bible-based books with the first chapter of each book free for you to read. You can sign up to receive our free monthly newsletter either by mail or by email, to receive a daily Devotional from one of our Scripture Meditation Cards or a free weekly download of a Bible teaching.

Copyright 2012

Jack and Judy Hartman

No part of this book may be used or reproduced in any manner whatsoever without written permission from the publisher except in the case of brief quotations and articles of review. For more information regarding this book, please contact:

Jack and Judy Hartman
Lamplight Ministries Inc.
PO Box 1307
Dunedin, Florida 34697-2921

Telephone: 1-800-540-1597
FAX: 1-727-784-2980
Website: lamplight.net
Email: lamplight@lamplight.net

ISBN: 9780915445233
Library of Congress Control Number: 2012911110

Dedication

When we consider the people who best exemplify God's instructions for growing older, we think of our treasured friends Rev. George and Rhonda Malkmus, Dr. Olin and Myra Idol, and Paul and Ann Malkmus. We dedicate this book to you. We thank you for spreading the message, "You Don't Have to Be Sick!" You are vibrant and alive in the Lord Jesus Christ. Thank you for pouring yourselves into the lives of people who want to go *Back to the Garden* (your monthly newsletter).

George, Rhonda, Olin, Myra, Paul and Ann, we love you and thank God for the blessing you are in our lives and in the lives of millions of people all over the world.

We each began studying the Bible in the *King James Version*. If we could write this entire book with the *King James Version*, we would. However, we want to present the reader with the best possible explanation of each verse of Scripture.

We have reviewed each verse of Scripture in this book to prayerfully select the Bible version that we believe will help you to best understand what God is saying to you. In some cases we have used *The New International Version* (NIV) when we believe the language in this particular passage of Scripture will give you more comprehension. In other cases we have used *The Amplified Bible* (AMP) when we believe the amplification will explain more to you.

The *King James Version* (KJV) of the Bible received its name from King James who was the king of England from 1603 to 1625. King James is considered to have been one of the most intellectual and learned kings in the history of Great Britain. He is primarily remembered for authorizing the production of the *King James Version* of the Bible. This English translation from Greek and Hebrew is the most printed book in the history of the world with more than one billion copies in print.

The New International Version (NIV) is the result of the study of a group of approximately 100 Hebrew and Greek scholars representing more than 20 denominations. This team of scholars devoted 10 years to complete the NIV translation. The goal of this committee was to faithfully translate the original Greek, Hebrew and Aramaic biblical text into clearly understandable English. The NIV is the most widely purchased contemporary Bible today.

The Amplified Bible is the result of the study of a group of Bible scholars who spent a total of more than 20,000 hours amplifying the Bible. They believe that traditional word-by-word translation often fails to reveal the shades of meaning that are part of the original Greek, Hebrew and Aramaic biblical texts.

Any amplification of the original text uses brackets for words that clarify the meaning and parentheses for words that contain additional phrases included in the original language. Through this amplification the reader will gain a better understanding of what Hebrew and Greek listeners instinctively understood.

Scripture quotations marked (KJV) are taken from the *King James Version* of the Bible.

Scripture quotations marked (NIV) are taken from *The Holy Bible, New International Version,* copyright 1973, 1978, 1984 by International Bible Society. Used by permission of Zondervan Publishing House.

Scripture quotations marked (AMP) are taken from *The Amplified Bible*, Old Testament, copyright 1965, 1987 by the Zondervan Corporation, Grand Rapids Michigan, or *The Amplified Bible*, New Testament, copyright 1954, 1958, 1987 by the Lockman Foundation, LaHabra, California. Used by permission.

TABLE OF CONTENTS

Introduction 29
1. Your Father Promises to Carry You from Birth to Death 31
2. Offset Physical Deterioration in Your Body 35
3. You Must Turn Away from the World 41
4. The Word of God Is Filled with the Power of God 47
5. Meditate Day and Night on the Word of God 53
6. How Do You Meditate on the Word of God? 59
7. Fill Your Mind and Your Heart with the Word of God .. 67
8. God Has Provided You with Powerful Spiritual Medicine 73
9. Focus Continually on God and His Word 79
10. Your Life Belongs to Jesus Christ 85
11. God Lives in Your Heart 91
12. Quiet and Confident Trust in God 97
13. God Will Bring You Safely through Adversity 103
14. Increase Your Faith in God As You Grow Older 107
15. God's Instructions Regarding the Past and the Future 113
16. Trust God to Guide You One Day at a Time 117
17. God Has a Specific Plan for Your Life 123
18. Focus Fervently on God's Assignment for Your Life ... 129
19. Deep Fulfillment from Being in Partnership with God 135
20. Be Careful What You Are Hearing 139
21. God's Instructions for Health and Healing 145
22. A Simple and Effective Way to Exercise 151
23. The Physical and Psychological Benefits of Exercise .. 159

24. The Hallelujah Diet 167
25. An Effective Method to Increase Your Energy 171
26. You Should Not Be Afraid of Death 179
27. Every Christian Is a Citizen of Heaven 183
28. There Is No Pain or Sorrow in Heaven 189
Conclusion 195
Appendix 197
Study Guide 203

Introduction

I (Jack) am 80 years old as this book goes to the printer. Judy is the co-author of this book. She is 73 years old. We will share many verses of Scripture with you that will show you exactly what your Father instructs you to do to age successfully. We also will share many lessons that we have learned from personal experience that we believe will help you as you grow older.

Do not fear growing old. Your loving Father has given you specific instructions pertaining to the final years of your life. All that He asks is for you to study His Word, to learn His instructions and to faithfully obey these instructions.

Your final years on earth are a unique period in your life. These years often are very different from the preceding years. Your Father does not want you to struggle and strain during this stage of your life.

Robert Browning, a 19th century English poet, said, "Grow old along with me. The best is yet to be." The final years of your life can be your best years if you will live these years the way your Father has instructed you to live.

The instructions from the Word of God should be invaluable to you. The instructions from us are purely discretionary. We will be very careful not to hold ourselves up as experts. We believe that some of the things we have learned from experience will help many people who read this book.

You will make many decisions that will affect the length and quality of your life. If you will carefully examine and obey God's instructions and consider our suggestions and use whatever you can, we believe that you will be able to escape many of the problems that some people experience as they grow older. If you learn how to age successfully, the final years before you go to heaven can be the best years of your life.

Chapter 1

Your Father Promises to Carry You from Birth to Death

Your Father's incredible love for you is much greater than you can comprehend with the limitations of human understanding. God wants to help you during the final years of your life. He said, "…you who have been borne by Me from your birth, carried from the womb: Even to your old age I am He, and even to hair white with age will I carry you…." (Isaiah 46:3-4 AMP)

God explains that He will carry you from the day you were born through your old age. There is no question that your loving Father desires to bring you safely through every year of your life, including the final years of your life.

If you are a senior citizen and you are struggling in any way, meditate consistently on this magnificent promise from God. Open your mouth as you meditate and say something like, "My Father has promised to carry me every day of my life from the time I was born up to the time that I go to heaven. Thank You, dear Father, for carrying me during these final years of my life."

Allow your ears to hear your mouth continually speaking this glorious promise from God. Be encouraged by this wonderful promise from your loving Father. Have absolute faith that He *will* carry you through your final years of your life to the degree that you know this specific promise, have faith in this promise and do your very best to learn and obey God's specific instructions pertaining to your final years on earth.

You may look at this promise and wonder how God can make this promise when you have seen other people experience tremendous adversity during the final years of their lives. God's promises are conditional. Your Father always does what He says He will do. You must do your part. Your part is to learn and obey God's specific instructions that tell you exactly how He wants you to live as you grow older.

Are you humble and teachable? *Will you* do your very best to learn and obey all of the specific instructions that your Father has given to you? God promises to bless His children who are obedient (see James 1:25). He also says that He resists people who are proud and that He gives grace to the humble (see I Peter 5:5). God resists people who are proud because they are doing things their way, not His way.

Do not block your Father from carrying you throughout your life because of your ignorance of or disobedience to the specific instructions He has given to you. If you will do your very best to learn and obey God's instructions pertaining to your final years on earth, you can be absolutely certain that He *will* carry you right up to the day that you go to be with Him in heaven.

The Word of God explains the normal lifespan of a human being. "The days of our years are threescore years and ten (seventy years) – or even, if by reason of strength, fourscore years (eighty years)…" (Psalm 90:10 AMP)

Does this mean that you can only expect to live until age 80? No, it does not. The Bible says that Moses lived much longer than the age of 80. "…Moses was an hundred and twenty years old when he died: his eye was not dim, nor his natural force abated." (Deuteronomy 34:7 KJV)

Moses lived to be 120 years old. Even at that advanced age, his eyesight was excellent and his health was good. Make the quality decision that you will learn the instructions your Father has given you to obey as you grow older.

You can see that your Father has promised to carry you throughout your life. Every promise in the Word of God is completely reliable. "God is faithful (reliable, trustworthy, and therefore ever true to His promise, and He can be depended on)..." (I Corinthians 1:9 AMP)

If God says that He will carry you throughout old age, you can be absolutely certain that He will do what He promises. Trust God completely.

Bernard Baruch was a successful financier and an advisor to many senior government officials. He once said, "To me, old age is always 15 years older than I am." Mr. Baruch never looked at himself as being old.

Ralph Waldo Emerson was a 19th century American author and poet. He once said, "We don't count a man's years until he has nothing else to count."

Henry Wadsworth Longfellow was a 19th century American poet and educator. Mr. Longfellow once said, "Age is youth itself, though in another dress."

There is no question that your Father wants you to live a long and a full life. He wants you to be so humble and teachable that you will consistently turn to His Word to learn His specific instructions. If you do, the following words that King Solomon spoke to his son are your Father's promise to you. "Hear, O my son, and receive my sayings; and the years of thy life shall be many." (Proverbs 4:10 KJV)

You *will* enjoy long life *if* you will learn and obey God's specific instructions. King Solomon also said, "My son, forget not my law or teaching, but let your heart keep my commandments; for length of days and years of a life [worth living] and tranquility [inward and outward and continuing through old age till death], these shall they add to you." (Proverbs 3:1-2 AMP)

This verse and the amplification says that, if you will faithfully obey God's instructions, you *will* enjoy a long and a full life. This verse and the amplification go on to explain that you will receive supernatural tranquility from God throughout your old age up until the time that you die *if* you learn and obey God's instructions.

There is no question that your Father wants you to enjoy a long, full and peaceful life. If you truly love God, you will learn and obey His instructions (see I John 5:3). "…love the Lord your God, obey His voice, and cling to Him. For He is your life and the length of your days…" (Deuteronomy 30:20 AMP)

You are instructed to cling to God. Stay close to your loving Father throughout every day of your life. If He is at the absolute center of your life and every aspect of your life revolves around Him, you will receive the long life that His Word consistently promises to you. "For by me [Wisdom from God] your days shall be multiplied, and the years of your life shall be increased." (Proverbs 9:11 AMP)

God promises to give you wisdom so that you will live a long and a full life. "The reverent and worshipful fear of the Lord prolongs one's days, but the years of the wicked shall be made short." (Proverbs 10:27 AMP)

When you fear God, you revere Him and hold Him in constant awe. If you truly fear and revere God, you will live a long life. People who do not revere God and obey His instructions often will find that their lives are cut short.

This chapter contains several specific promises and instructions from the Word of God that will enable you to live a long and a full life. The next chapter will explain several additional instructions from God pertaining to long life.

Chapter 2

Offset Physical Deterioration in Your Body

As many people grow older, their bodies begin to fail them to varying degrees. God tells you exactly what you should do if this takes place. "...Though our outer man is [progressively] decaying and wasting away, yet our inner self is being [progressively] renewed day after day." (II Corinthians 4:16 AMP)

The words "outer man" in this verse refer to your body. When this verse speaks of "progressively decaying and wasting away," it refers to the worsening of physical health that some people experience as their bodies give them problems as they grow older.

Before we comment further on this verse, we want to point out that this decaying and wasting away does not necessarily happen to every person. In the last chapter you saw that Moses lived to the age of 120 and that he was in excellent physical condition at that age. We want to emphasize that a decline in physical health is not automatic. The choices that we make can either delay or hasten the breakdown of the body.

There is no question that many people are experiencing decay in their bodies as they grow older. In almost every case, this deterioration comes about because of a series of choices that these individuals made during their lives in regard to failure to exercise, the food that they ate and other choices that caused their bodies to age prematurely.

If your body is aging and deteriorating, this verse of Scripture tells you exactly what God instructs you to do. God tells you that your "inner self" should be "progressively renewed *day after day*."

Please note that the word "progressively" is used two times in the amplification of this verse. If your body is progressively decaying, you must offset this deterioration by progressively renewing your mind in God's Word "day after day." *Are you* renewing your mind in God's Word *every* day?

The words "outer man" in II Corinthians 4:16 refer to your body. Anyone who looks at you can see your body. The words "inner self" refer to the part of you that people cannot see. The Bible calls this "...the hidden person of the heart..." (I Peter 3:4 AMP)

The *real you* is the hidden person who lives in your heart. As your body grows older, you must understand the vital importance of progressively renewing the hidden person of the heart. You must be made new on the inside as you grow older on the outside.

The Bible gives you specific instruction on how to renew this hidden person. "Strip yourselves of your former nature [put off and discard your old unrenewed self] which characterized your previous manner of life and becomes corrupt through lusts and desires that spring from delusion; and be constantly renewed in the spirit of your mind [having a fresh mental and spiritual attitude], and put on the new nature (the regenerate self) created in God's image, [Godlike] in true righteousness and holiness." (Ephesians 4:22-24 AMP)

This passage of Scripture instructs you to strip yourself of the way that you used to be before you started renewing your mind in God's Word. This verse speaks of "lusts and desires that spring from delusion." If you do not obey God's instructions to renew your mind in His Word every day, you will be susceptible to the lusts and desires of the unrenewed self that cause your body to age and decay prematurely.

God is very specific about how often you should renew your mind by studying His Word. You saw in II Corinthians 4:16 that God instructs you to renew your mind "*day after day*." Ephesians

4:23 instructs you to "be *constantly* renewed in the spirit of your mind."

Every Christian should renew his or her mind in God's Word on a daily basis. If your body is aging and wasting away, you *must* offset what is taking place in your body by consistently renewing your mind by studying God's Word.

The amplification in Ephesians 4:22-24 tells you what will happen if you consistently renew your mind in God's Word. You will "have a fresh mental and spiritual attitude." You will "put on the new nature" that you received when Jesus Christ became your Savior.

When God created you, He created you in His image (see Genesis 1:27). God made you like He is. When you were regenerated spiritually through receiving Jesus as your Savior, you received a new nature deep down inside of yourself. This new nature will not grow and mature automatically. You will become more and more like God to the degree that you consistently renew your mind in His Word.

You must understand the vital importance of renewing your mind in the Word of God each and every day as you grow older. "Do not be conformed to this world (this age), [fashioned after and adapted to its external, superficial customs], but be transformed (changed) by the [entire] renewal of your mind [by its new ideals and its new attitude], so that you may prove [for yourselves] what is the good and acceptable and perfect will of God, even the thing which is good and acceptable and perfect [in His sight for you]." (Romans 12:2 AMP)

This verse emphasizes that you should not conform to the ways of the world. You should consistently turn away from the ways of the world. Turning away from the world becomes increasingly important as you grow older, particularly if your body is decaying.

The amplification in this verse explains how superficial the ways of the world are. Your Father explains that your life will be *transformed* if you consistently renew your mind in His Word.

The Greek word "metamorphoo" is translated as "transformed" in this verse. The English word "metamorphis" that means a complete change comes from this same Greek word. Your life will be completely changed *if* you faithfully obey your Father's instructions to renew your mind by studying His Word each day. As you renew your mind in God's Word, you will come more and more into God's perfect will for your life.

Many Christians do *not* renew their minds in God's Word each day as God has specifically instructed His children to do. These Christians often do not pay any immediate penalty for their ignorance of or disobedience to God's instructions. They do not understand the problems that they will bring upon themselves in their later years if they do not faithfully obey God's instructions to renew their minds in His Word each and every day.

As you grow older, you must understand the vital importance of not making any exceptions to your Father's instructions to renew your mind in His Word each day. A time will come in the lives of many older people when their bodies will prevail and pull them down because they have not obeyed God's instructions to consistently renew their minds in His Word.

Your Father wants you to see life from His perspective, not from a worldly perspective. Your Father has promised to transform your thinking from the world's ways to His way if you will faithfully obey His instructions to renew your mind in His Word. "With the aged [you say] is wisdom, and with length of days comes understanding." (Job 12:12 AMP)

This verse of Scripture speaks of the wisdom and understanding that comes to older people. This wisdom and understanding does not come automatically. You will receive wisdom and understanding from God if you consistently renew your mind in His Word. "Get wisdom, get understanding; do not forget my words or turn away from them. Do not forsake wisdom, and she will protect you; love her, and she will watch over you." (Proverbs 4:5-6 NIV)

Some older people resist change. They are set in their ways. If you faithfully obey your Father's instructions to renew your mind in His Word each day, your thinking will be flexible and resilient. You will be able to deal with challenges in your old age that you otherwise would not be able to cope with.

Do not allow your mind to be idle as many elderly people do. Someone once said, "The idle mind is the devil's workshop." You should fill your mind consistently with the supernatural power of the living Word of God (see Hebrews 4:12).

Your Father has given you the ability to direct your thoughts. He has given you the ability to program your mind with His Word. As you grow older, your Father wants you to think more and more the way that He thinks and less and less the way the world thinks. "My thoughts are not your thoughts, neither are your ways My ways, says the Lord. For as the heavens are higher than the earth, so are My ways higher than your ways and My thoughts than your thoughts." (Isaiah 55:8-9 AMP)

God's ways are much higher and very different from the ways of the world. *If* you obey God's instructions to consistently renew your mind in His Word, you will think more and more like God thinks. You will be much better equipped to cope with the challenges that many people face during the final years of their lives.

How do you renew your mind each day in the Word of God? We will not attempt to give you a detailed answer to this question here. You might want to refer to our book, *How to Study the Bible*. This book was written almost 30 years ago. Nevertheless, the scriptural instructions in this book have not changed. God's Word never changes (see Psalm 119:96).

You will note in the front of this book comments from people pertaining to *How to Study the Bible*. If you turn to these comments, you will see that a man from England, a husband and wife in Idaho and a man from Tennessee benefitted greatly from reading this book. These are just three of many comments that we have received on this book (see our website: www. lamplight.net).

There are many ways to study the Bible. Our way is not the only way. However, we do recommend the other 23 books and the 10 sets of Scripture Meditation Cards that we have written. You will see a listing of these books and cards in the front of this book and an order form in the back of this book.

Each of our books is devoted to a specific topic. If you want to learn what the Bible says about patience and perseverance, quiet confidence in the Lord, praying effectively, overcoming fear, drawing closer to God or receiving God's joy, our books will give you scriptural instructions in these areas. If you want to learn how to walk in victory over adversity, to receive healing, to increase your faith in God, to receive God's perfect peace, to receive God's wisdom or to increase your energy and vitality, you will see that we have written books on each of these topics. We also have written Scripture Meditation Cards on ten of these topics.

If you are interested in studying God's Word in any of the areas covered by our publications, we have done the work for you. We have looked up a large number of Scripture references on each of these topics. We have broken this Scripture down into subcategories. Each Scripture reference is explained in simple and easy-to-understand language. You *can* renew your mind by consistently studying the Scripture references contained in our books and Scripture cards.

Chapter 3

You Must Turn Away from the World

In the last chapter we briefly mentioned God's instructions to turn away from the external and superficial customs of the world. In this chapter we will look into God's Word for more instructions in this area. "Do not love or cherish the world or the things that are in the world. If anyone loves the world, love for the Father is not in him. For all that is in the world – the lust of the flesh [craving for sensual gratification] and the lust of the eyes [greedy longings of the mind] and the pride of life [assurance in one's own resources or in the stability of earthly things] – these do not come from the Father but are from the world [itself]." (I John 2:15-16 AMP)

Your loving Father says that you should not love the world or the ways of the world. If you love the things of the world, you do *not* love God. Worldly attractions, no matter how good and harmless they may seem, do not come from God.

The amplification instructs you not to crave gratification of your senses. You should never lust after anything that you can see with your eyes. As you grow older, you may face some of the significant problems that many older people experience. You should not trust completely in yourself or worldly sources to bring you through.

You saw in the last chapter that the world's ways are very different from God's ways (see Isaiah 55:8-9). Just because something seems right from a worldly perspective does not mean that this is what God desires. God said, "There is a way which seems right to a man and appears straight before him, but at the end of it is the way of death." (Proverbs 14:12 AMP)

Many times things that seem right from a worldly perspective will lead you to spiritual death. God often emphasizes through repetition. Please note that God says virtually the same thing in a subsequent verse in Proverbs. "There is a way that seems right to a man and appears straight before him, but at the end of it is the way of death." (Proverbs 16:25 AMP)

Why did God say the same thing in two different verses of Proverbs? God is *emphasizing* that doing what seems right to you often is "the way of death." If you do what seems right from a worldly perspective, your thoughts, words and actions often will lead you to spiritual death and sometimes to premature physical death. *If* you have paid the price of renewing your mind daily in God's Word, you will know that things that seem right from a worldly perspective often are not God's ways.

When you renew your mind each day by studying God's Word, you are *programming* your mind with God's instructions and promises. You will be spiritually alive instead of experiencing the spiritual death that you will experience if your mind consistently has been programmed by the ways of the world. This discernment between God's ways and the world's ways is very important at any stage of your life, but renewing your mind in God's Word is increasingly important as you grow older.

Your Father wants you to learn and to live your life *His way* instead of doing things the world's way because they seem right to you. Andrew Murray, a South African writer, teacher and pastor, once said, "Shut the world out, withdraw from all worldly thoughts and occupations and shut yourself in alone with God."

As you grow older, you must understand the importance of turning away from the world and turning toward God. "...Do you not know that being the world's friend is being God's enemy? So whoever chooses to be a friend of the world takes his stand as an enemy of God." (James 4:4 AMP)

You have seen that your loving Father has promised to carry you throughout your life from birth until death. However, if you are worldly in your thinking, you actually become an enemy of God. Your unrenewed worldly thinking often will *block* God from carrying you the way that He wants to carry you through your old age.

One of the best ways to effectively turn away from the ways of the world is to consistently renew your mind in God's Word. If you learn and obey God's specific instructions throughout the final years of your life, you will make one of the most important decisions that you could possibly make.

The Word of God should have a high priority during the final years of your life. God said, "...this is the man to whom I will look and have regard: he who is humble and of a broken or wounded spirit, and who trembles at My word and reveres My commands." (Isaiah 66:2 AMP)

Do you want God to "look to you and have regard for you?" Of course you do. God will carry you during the final years of your life if you truly are humble and if you tremble at His Word and revere His commands.

Why would you *tremble* at the Word of God? You should tremble at the Word of God because of your absolute certainty that the Word of God is filled with the supernatural power of God. Do you *revere* God's instructions just as you revere Him? Are you like the psalmist who said, "...my heart stands in awe of Your words..." (Psalm 119:161 AMP)

You should be in absolute awe of the Word of God. "...the Word that God speaks is alive and full of power [making it active, operative, energizing, and effective]; it is sharper than any two-edged sword, penetrating to the dividing line of the breath of life (soul) and [the immortal] spirit, and of joints and marrow [of the deepest parts of our nature], exposing and sifting and analyzing and judging the very thoughts and purposes of the heart." (Hebrews 4:12 AMP)

The Bible is spiritually alive. It is filled with the power of God. The amplification of this verse says that God's Word is able to energize you and to make your life effective. God's Word is able to penetrate between your soul and spirit to show you exactly what you are like deep down inside of yourself.

The older you are, the more humble and teachable you should be. You should have a hunger to come to God each day to learn from His Word. A humble and teachable attitude is vitally important at all times in your life, but this humble attitude is especially important during the final years of your life. "…Clothe (apron) yourselves, all of you, with humility [as the garb of a servant, so that its covering cannot possibly be stripped from you, with freedom from pride and arrogance] toward one another. For God sets Himself against the proud (the insolent, the overbearing, the disdainful, the presumptuous, the boastful) – [and He opposes, frustrates, and defeats them], but gives grace (favor, blessing) to the humble." (I Peter 5:5 AMP)

This verse explains the vital importance of being humble. You are instructed to "clothe yourself with humility" so that nothing can strip your humility from you. You must *not* be proud. This verse tells you that God dislikes pride *so much* that He "sets Himself against" people who consistently are proud. The amplification says that God actually "opposes, frustrates and defeats" people who are proud. You then are told that God "gives grace, favor and blessing *to the humble*."

Do you want God to set Himself against you, to oppose you and to frustrate you and to defeat you during the final years of your life? Of course you don't. God does not want to treat you this way either, but pride forces Him to do this.

Your Father wants to give grace to you continually during the final years of your life because you are humble, teachable and obedient. Do not block God by being so proud that you ignore His repeated instructions to consistently renew your mind in His Word. "Study and be eager and do your utmost to present yourself to God approved (tested by trial), a workman who has no cause to be ashamed, correctly analyzing and accurately dividing [rightly handling and skillfully teaching] the Word of Truth." (II Timothy 2:15 AMP)

This verse tells you that God will approve what you are doing *if* you study His Word eagerly and if you work hard at your daily Bible study. You will win God's approval if you work so diligently at your daily Bible study that you have no reason to be ashamed. *Do you* believe that God approves of your daily Bible study? *Are you* obeying His specific instructions to renew your mind in His Word each and every day?

I (Jack) do not believe that I would be alive today at the age of 80 if I had not consistently renewed my mind in God's Word and meditated day and night on the holy Scriptures for more than 35 years. I cannot get enough of the Word of God. The more I get, the more I want.

You must understand the vital importance of living your life based upon your heart being filled with God's Word instead of focusing on the external things of the world. "…the Lord sees not as man sees; for man looks on the outward appearance, but the Lord looks on the heart." (I Samuel 16:7 AMP)

Your Father wants you to look at yourself the same way that He looks at you. Instead of focusing on your body and your external appearance, you should focus continually on the hidden person of your heart deep down inside of yourself (see I Peter 3:4).

Some older people spend a significant amount of time, energy and money attempting to cover up external signs of aging. These people dye their hair, wear wigs, have plastic surgery and do other things in an attempt to make themselves look younger.

We are not saying that you should not present a neat and presentable appearance. We are saying that you should not spend large amounts of time, energy and money on your external appearance instead of focusing on what you truly are deep down inside of yourself.

Older people should not identify with their appearance. Your hair may have turned white. Your hair may be thinning or gone. You undoubtedly have some wrinkles. However, God's Word clearly instructs you to focus on the inner you, *not* on your external appearance. Focus continually on the hidden person of the heart. Keep the hidden person of your heart young by consistently renewing your mind in God's supernatural living Word.

Chapter 4

The Word of God Is Filled with the Power of God

You have seen what the Bible teaches about the vital importance of renewing your mind if your body is decaying. You must renew your mind as you grow older so that you will be able to understand what God instructs you to do during the final years of your life. This book contains many verses of Scripture that explain exactly what your Father instructs you to do during the final years of your life.

If you renew your mind daily with these specific verses of Scripture, you will be studying exactly what your Father wants you to study as you grow older. In this chapter we will look carefully at the holy Scriptures to learn additional truths about the Word of God.

Every word in the Bible comes from God Himself. The Bible is supernatural. It is completely different from books that are written by human beings because of the following statement. "Every Scripture is God-breathed (given by His inspiration)..." (II Timothy 3:16 AMP)

If you faithfully obey your Father's instructions to renew your mind in His Word each day, you can be certain that you are renewing your mind in the Book of Instructions that God has provided for you. God supernaturally inspired the writing of each human author of the Bible.

The apostle Paul explained this great spiritual truth in his letter to the Thessalonians when he said, "…you received the message of God [which you heard] from us, you welcomed it not as the word of [mere] men, but as it truly is, the Word of God, which is effectually at work in you who believe [exercising its superhuman power in those who adhere to and trust in and rely on it]." (I Thessalonians 2:13 AMP)

These words that God spoke through Paul when He anointed Paul's message to the people of Thessalonica also apply to your life today. The Bible is *not* the "word of mere men." The Bible "truly is the Word of God." The Bible is filled with the supernatural power of God. God's power will work effectively in your life *if* you will learn and have absolute faith and trust and reliance on God's promises.

No book written by any human being can *remotely* compare with the Bible. "…everything [human] has its limits and end [no matter how extensive, noble, and excellent]; but Your commandment is exceedingly broad and extends without limits [into eternity]." (Psalm 119:96 AMP)

All of the books that we write have value only because each book is filled with the Word of God. The remainder of each book consists primarily of our explanation of the verses of Scripture that we are studying.

The Bible is eternal. The words that you study if you renew your mind in God's Word each day will have eternal consequences. If you learn how to consistently get these words into your mind and your heart, you will take the Word of God that is in you to heaven. "…the Truth which lives and stays on in our hearts and will be with us forever" (II John 1:2 AMP)

You have just seen that both Psalm 119:96 and II John 1:2 explain that the Word of God is eternal. God has anointed the human authors of the Bible with supernatural instructions that you will need throughout your life on earth.

The Bible is a spiritual fountain of youth. The Word of God can and will keep the hidden person of your heart young and vibrant spiritually as your physical body grows older. You will not identify with the decreased energy in your body if you energize yourself each and every day with God's Word as your Father has instructed you to do. "...we possess this precious treasure [the divine Light of the Gospel] in [frail, human] vessels of earth, that the grandeur and exceeding greatness of the power may be shown to be from God and not from ourselves." (II Corinthians 4:7 AMP)

The Bible is a wonderful treasure that you did not earn and do not deserve. Your Father has given you His Word because of His grace and His incredible love for you. The amplification of this verse explains that the Bible is filled with "the divine Light" of God. If you will faithfully obey your Father's instructions to renew your mind in His Word each day, God's supernatural spiritual light will shine deep down inside of you. You will be able to understand great spiritual truths that definitely will affect your final years on earth.

This verse and the amplification explain that you are a "frail, human vessel." The Word of God is filled with the power of God. You must learn how to consistently get the supernatural power of God up off the printed pages of the Bible into your mind and your heart. "...He has bestowed on us His precious and exceedingly great promises, so that through them you may escape [by flight] from the moral decay (rottenness and corruption) that is in the world because of covetousness (lust and greed), and become sharers (partakers) of the divine nature." (II Peter 1:4 AMP)

Your Father has given His supernatural promises to you. The Bible is God's gift to you. Receive this precious gift by making the quality decision to obey God's instructions to renew your mind in His Word each and every day throughout the remainder of your life.

Your Father has made it possible for you to "*escape* the moral decay, rottenness and corruption" that fills the world during these last days before Jesus Christ returns (see II Timothy 3:2-4). The world on the whole today is much more selfish and self-centered than ever before. If you learn how to consistently fill your mind and your heart with God's Word, you will partake of God's nature. You will become more and more like God.

Once again, renewing your mind is important at every stage of life, but this daily renewal is vitally important during the final years of your life. You learned in II Corinthians 4:16 in Chapter 2 that you must offset any progressive decay that is taking place in your body by renewing your mind daily in the supernatural living Word of God. "…I commend you to the Word of His grace [to the commands and counsels and promises of His unmerited favor]. It is able to build you up and to give you [your rightful] inheritance among all God's set-apart ones (those consecrated, purified, and transformed of soul)." (Acts 20:32 AMP)

Once again you are told that you are able to receive the supernatural blessings of the Word of God because of God's grace. You will receive God's instructions and promises of His unmerited favor to the degree that you are humble and teachable.

This verse and the amplification explain that the Word of God builds you up spiritually. The Word of God will give you the magnificent inheritance that was provided for you by the supernatural victory that Jesus Christ won for you when He died on the cross and subsequently rose from the dead (see John 16:33, Romans 8:37, II Corinthians 2:14 and I John 5:4-5).

Every person who has received Jesus Christ as his or her Savior will receive this great inheritance by living throughout eternity in the glory of heaven. You also will be blessed during your life on earth to the degree that you are "consecrated, purified and transformed of soul."

Receive the supernatural inheritance that God has provided for you during the final years of your life and after you die. "…all of us, as with unveiled face, [because we] continued to behold [in the Word of God] as in a mirror the glory of the Lord, are constantly being transfigured into His very own image in ever increasing splendor and from one degree of glory to another; [for this comes] from the Lord [Who is] the Spirit." (II Corinthians 3:18 AMP)

This verse and the amplification speak to all Christians who consistently behold God's glory as they renew their minds each day in His Word. If you study God's Word carefully, you will steadily become more and more like God.

Are you receiving this magnificent gift from God? *Are you* consistently becoming more and more like God because you renew your mind in His Word each day?

If you can even begin to comprehend the incredible supernatural power of the Word of God, you will not allow one day to go by during the remainder of your life when you do not fill your mind and your heart with God's Word. "Is not My word like fire [that consumes all that cannot endure the test]? says the Lord, and like a hammer that breaks in pieces the rock [of most stubborn resistance]?" (Jeremiah 23:29 AMP)

This verse and the amplification explain that, in the spiritual realm, the Word of God is like an all-consuming fire. You are told that the Word of God is like a powerful spiritual hammer that breaks up anything that resists you. Whatever problems you experience during the final years of your life can and will be overcome to the degree that God's Word lives inside of you.

In the first four chapters of this book we have talked primarily about renewing your mind in God's Word. In the next chapter we will look specifically at what God says about *meditating day and night* on His Word.

Chapter 5

Meditate Day and Night on the Word of God

You have seen the vital importance of renewing your *mind* in the Word of God each day as you grow older. We now are ready to learn how to get God's Word from your *mind* down into your *heart*. The following instructions were given directly from God to Joshua when he succeeded Moses as the leader of Israel. God said, "This Book of the Law shall not depart out of your mouth, but you shall meditate on it day and night, that you may observe and do according to all that is written in it. For then you shall make your way prosperous, and then you shall deal wisely and have good success." (Joshua 1:8 AMP)

These instructions that God gave to Joshua also apply to you. We believe that this verse of Scripture is extremely important. We have included it in almost every one of the 24 Christian books we have written. We will begin by studying the last part of this verse first. God promises that *"you* shall make your way prosperous." He also promises that *"you* shall deal wisely and have good success."

The word "prosperous" in this verse means more than just financial prosperity. The Hebrew word "tsalach" that is translated as "prosperous" here means "to press forward, break out and go over."

This word does include financial prosperity. It also means that *you* will be able to push forward, break out and go over the problems that you face during the final years of your life. You will be able to deal wisely with whatever challenges you face if you meditate day and night on the Word of God. You will receive supernatural wisdom from God (see James 1:5-8) if you consistently meditate on His Word.

This verse also says that you will have good success. The Bible contains more than 500,000 words. *Strong's Exhaustive Concordance,* which contains every word in the Bible, has the word "success" only *one* time – in Joshua 1:8.

If you want to be successful at any time of your life, and especially during the final years of your life, you must obey the instructions that God gives you in the first part of this verse. First, He tells you that His Word "shall not depart out of your mouth." If you want to receive these supernatural blessings from God, you should *speak* His Word consistently during each day and night of your life.

God instructs you to meditate day and night on His Word. The Hebrew word "hagah" that is translated as "meditate" here means "to ponder and to speak." When you ponder as you meditate on Scripture, you weigh what you are thinking about. You turn God's instruction or promise over and over in your mind. You contemplate what you are pondering. You absorb it.

You open your mouth and speak what you are pondering about. You do this consistently every day and night of your life. You are instructed to do this consistent Scripture meditation so that you will "observe and do according to all that is written in it."

We now are ready to study another passage of Scripture that is included in most of our books. "...his delight and desire are in the law of the Lord, and on His law (the precepts, the instructions, the teachings of God) he habitually meditates (ponders and studies) by day and by night. And he shall be like a tree firmly planted [and tended] by the streams of water, ready to bring forth its fruit in its season; its leaf also shall not fade or wither; and everything he does shall prosper [and come to maturity]." (Psalm 1:2-3 AMP)

If you delight in the Word of God, you will not be able to get enough of God's Word. The more of God's Word you get, the more you will desire. You will habitually meditate day and night on the Word of God.

The amplification says that you "ponder and study" when you meditate on God's Word. Once again, when you ponder, you think deeply about what God is telling you in whatever passage of Scripture you are meditating on.

If you have a fervent delight and desire for God's Word and you habitually ponder day and night on what your Father is saying to you, you will be like a tree next to a stream of water that will always bring forth fruit even in a drought. You are told that *everything* you do will prosper.

Once again the same Hebrew word "tsalach" that was used in Joshua 1:8 is used here. If you meditate day and night on God's Word, you will be able to push forward, break out and go over many of the problems that you will face as you grow older.

Why would the leaves of a tree that is planted next to a stream of water never fade or wither? If a tree that is planted next to a stream experiences a severe drought and several weeks go by without rain, this tree still will produce fruit. The roots of the tree are able to reach down into the stream to bring up water when rain does not come down from the sky.

If you habitually meditate on the Word of God, you will consistently bear fruit in your life. We are talking in this book about the final years of your life. You must understand the vital importance of delighting *so much* in God's Word that you *will* meditate day and night on the holy Scriptures. You have seen in Joshua 1:8 and Psalm 1:2-3 that your Father promises that He will bless you abundantly if you meditate day and night on His Word.

Some people become increasingly pessimistic as they grow older. Your Father wants you to be just the opposite. He wants you to *fill* your eyes, your ears, your mind, your heart and your mouth day and night with the supernatural power of His Word. If you do, you will become increasingly optimistic, regardless of the problems you face.

We have explained that, when you meditate on Scripture, you *speak* the verses that you are meditating on. The more that you speak the promises and instructions your Father has given to you, the more you will understand what your Father is telling you and the stronger your faith in Him will be.

You learned from Hebrews 4:12 in Chapter 3 that the Word of God is supernaturally alive and filled with the power of God. If you faithfully obey your Father's instructions to meditate day and night on His Word, the Holy Spirit will quicken God's Word to you. You will understand much more than you could otherwise. God said, "Give ear, O my people, to my teaching; incline your ears to the words of my mouth." (Psalm 78:1 AMP)

Your Father speaks specifically about your *ears* in this verse. You are instructed to incline your ears toward God's supernatural Word. You should fill your ears continually with the Word of God. God said, "…all My words that I shall speak to you, receive in your heart and hear with your ears." (Ezekiel 3:10 AMP)

The word "all" in this verse is very important. Your Father wants you to work hard to find every possible Scripture reference that applies to whatever problem you face at any given time (see our book, *What Does God Say?* that contains 1,221 verses of Scripture on 94 topics). He then wants you to meditate day and night on this carefully selected Scripture so that *your* ears will hear *your* voice speaking His Word. Jesus said, "Whoever is of God listens to God. [Those who belong to God hear the words of God.]…" (John 8:47 AMP)

Is Jesus Christ your Savior? If He is, you are of God. You belong to God. You are instructed to *listen* to God. Your ears must *hear* the Word of God continually as you obey God's instructions to meditate day and night on His Word. Jesus said, "He who has ears to hear, let him be listening and let him consider and perceive and comprehend by hearing." (Matthew 11:15 AMP)

Jesus explains that you comprehend and understand God's Word when you hear it. The more *your ears* hear *your mouth* speaking God's Word, the more you will understand what your Father is saying to you. "Incline your ear [submit and consent to the divine will] and come to Me; hear, and your soul will revive…" (Isaiah 55:3 AMP)

Once again you are instructed to incline your ears to what God is saying to you. If you consistently *hear* what God is saying to you as you speak His Word while you meditate on it, you will obey God's instructions. You will draw closer to God. If you obey these instructions, your soul will *revive*. These instructions apply to every time in your life, but they are especially important during the final years of your life.

If you are experiencing problems with your health or in any other area, you should *fill* your ears continually with God's supernatural living Word. Jesus said, "…Blessed (happy and to be envied) rather are those who hear the Word of God and obey and practice it!" (Luke 11:28 AMP)

Something supernatural happens when you consistently hear God's Word and do what your Father instructs you to do. "…faith comes by hearing [what is told], and what is heard comes by the preaching [of the message that came from the lips] of Christ (the Messiah Himself)." (Romans 10:17 AMP)

Please note that the words "hearing" and "heard" in this verse. Your faith in God will increase when you hear anointed pastors and teachers teaching the Word of God. However, you will find that your faith in God will increase much more rapidly when *your ears* consistently hear *your mouth* boldly speaking God's promises as you meditate day and night on His Word. Instead of talking about whatever problems you face as you grow older, you should *speak* God's Word.

The Bible does *not* say that faith in God comes from *having heard* the Word of God. The Bible says that faith comes from *hearing* the Word of God. You should pour God's Word into your eyes and your ears every day and night of your life as you faithfully meditate on the holy Scriptures.

Your faith in God will increase when your ears consistently hear the Word of God. The opposite also is true. Doubt, unbelief, worry and fear also will increase if your ears consistently hear your mouth speaking about the problems you face. As you grow older, you should focus continually on saying what God says instead of repeatedly talking about the seeming severity of whatever problems you face.

The Greek word "akoa" that is translated as "hearing" in Romans 10:17 literally means "to understand what you hear." The more that your ears hear your mouth speaking God's Word, the more you will understand what your loving Father is saying to you in whatever passage of Scripture you have chosen to meditate on.

Unfortunately, many older Christians go through the final years of their lives without *ever* hearing their mouths speaking God's promises and instructions. Many older Christians do not understand that they are missing out on a tremendous opportunity for their faith in God to increase consistently if they will faithfully obey God's instructions to meditate day and night on His Word.

Chapter 6

How Do You Meditate on the Word of God?

You have learned what God says about the importance of renewing your mind by studying His Word daily as you grow older. You have learned about the tremendous blessings that God promises to His children who faithfully meditate day and night on His Word. We now are ready to devote this chapter to show you how we recommend that you should meditate on the Word of God.

I (Jack) would like to begin this chapter by giving you an example of how I began to meditate on the Word of God. At the age of 43, the business that I had established several years earlier was on the verge of bankruptcy. Our business had been relatively successful in terms of gross sales, but I had borrowed so much money to build the business that my financial obligations far exceeded my ability to pay. Both my attorney and my accountant advised me to file bankruptcy.

Even though almost 38 years have gone by since that time, I can still remember the anguish that I went through. Bankruptcy was not as common then as it is now. All that I could think of was that I was about to lose the business I had worked so hard to build. I was concerned that we would lose the home we had purchased 12 years before. I was afraid that I would be unable to support my family and that we would have to move into a low-cost rental apartment.

I was on the verge of a nervous breakdown. I paced the floor at night. I couldn't sleep. All that I thought about was the seeming impossibility of solving the financial problems I faced. There did not seem to be any way out.

At that time a friend came to me and told me that there *was* a way out. He told me that the only way I would ever overcome these problems was to dedicate my life to Jesus Christ.

He explained that Jesus Christ came down from heaven as a human being to live on this earth for 33 years. He explained that Jesus died an agonizing death by crucifixion to pay the full price for all of my sins. He told me that I must believe in my heart and confess with my mouth that I would live throughout eternity in heaven because of the supreme sacrifice that Jesus made for me.

I had been brought up as a religious person. I attended Sunday School as a boy. I attended church until I was in college. Then I rebelled to some degree against my childhood upbringing. I stopped going to church on a regular basis, although I did go occasionally.

Because of the problems I faced, I devoured many positive-thinking type books. Several of these books contained Scripture references. I definitely was open to receiving Jesus Christ as my Savior.

My friend asked if I was ready to pray to receive Jesus as my Savior. I said that I was. He prayed a prayer that I repeated after him. In this prayer I admitted that I was a sinner. I said that I had absolute faith that Jesus Christ was the Son of God Who came down from heaven to pay the full price for all of my sins. I repented of my sins. I said that the only way I would live throughout eternity in the glory of heaven was because I was absolutely certain that Jesus had paid the full price for every sin I had ever committed.

I was born again spiritually on that day (see John 3:3-9 and Romans 10:9-10). This man then said the words that changed my life. He said, "Jack, you will never get out of this mess you are in unless you *saturate* yourself in the Word of God." He told me that every word in the Bible was inspired by God (see II Timothy 3:16).

At that time I knew nothing about the passages of Scripture that we explained in the last chapter about meditating day and night on the Word of God. The one verse of Scripture that I decided to start meditating on was Philippians 4:13. I meditated then on the *King James Version* of this verse because I did not know about *The Amplified Bible* at that time.

I would like to show you how I would meditate today on this same verse of Scripture from *The Amplified Bible*. We use *The Amplified Bible* more than any other version of the Bible in our books because it does what its title says it does – it amplifies. *The Amplified Bible* contains approximately 30% more words than the *King James Version, The NIV Bible* and other versions of the Bible.

I first started reading *The Amplified Bible* when I read a comment from Dr. Billy Graham saying that he often used this version of the Bible in his Bible study. As we stated at the beginning of this book, *The Amplified Bible* was written as the result of a group of Bible scholars who spent a total of more than 20,000 hours amplifying the Bible. These scholars believed that traditional word-by-word translation often fails to reveal shades of meaning that were part of the original Greek, Hebrew and Aramaic biblical texts.

All amplification of the original text uses brackets for words that clarify the meaning and parentheses for words that contain additional phrases included in the original Greek, Hebrew and Aramaic Bible texts. Through this amplification, the reader will gain a better understanding of what Hebrew and Greek listeners instinctively understood.

I now will meditate on Philippians 4:13 just as I would meditate today on this verse of Scripture as an 80-year-old man who faced difficult problems in his life. Here is this verse of Scripture. "I have strength for all things in Christ Who empowers me [I am ready for anything and equal to anything through Him Who infuses inner strength into me; I am self-sufficient in Christ's sufficiency]." (Philippians 4:13 AMP)

"Dear Father, this verse of Scripture says that I have strength for all things from Jesus Christ. The words "all things" include the problems that I now face. Thank You, Father, for providing me with supernatural strength from Jesus Christ that enables me to be ready for anything and equal to anything. I receive the strength that You have given to me, dear Jesus. Thank You for giving me this supernatural strength.

"I thank You that You are infusing inner strength into me. I know that You live in my heart because the Word of God says that You do. I know that You are strengthening me from the inside out so that I *will* be able to overcome this problem that I face."

This is how I would meditate on Philippians 4:13 from *The Amplified Bible*. When I meditate, I say what God says. I personalize it. My ears hear my mouth boldly speaking God's promises.

When I faced bankruptcy 38 years ago, I meditated continually on Philippians 4:13. I put this verse of Scripture and other verses that I found on 3x5 cards. I carried them with me continually. I also meditated often on 3x5 cards that were under a piece of plastic on my desk. I meditated on Scripture throughout the day and night for many months.

The business that seemed to face inevitable bankruptcy did *not* go bankrupt. Instead of continuing to be discouraged, I was constantly encouraged because of my consistent Scripture meditation. I had absolute faith that God would bring our business through this ordeal and He did.

I am retired from this business today. This business is very successful 38 years later. I thank God for honoring my constant Scripture meditation just as He said He would.

I have continued to meditate day and night on Scripture since that time. A Christian friend who has known me all of these years recently said to me, "Jack, a lot of people get into the Word of God when they are in trouble. You got into the Word of God when you were in trouble many years ago and you have never gotten out of it."

We started a small Bible study group in our office shortly after I became a Christian. This group consisted of four men and their wives. We began with general discussion. We did not have one specified teacher. The group soon agreed that I should be the teacher because of all of the time I had spent meditating on Scripture and the many verses of Scripture that I brought to our Bible study group.

I had been a Christian for less than two years when I began teaching this Bible study. I used massive amounts of Scripture that I had collected during my first two years as a Christian. What God did then was phenomenal. Once again, He honored my consistent Scripture meditation.

This small Bible study group in the conference room in our office soon outgrew the space. More than 30 people were coming to our conference room each Tuesday night. We went from there to a Holiday Inn. We then went to a Sheraton hotel. From there we had meetings in the cafeteria of a junior high school. From there we went to a high school auditorium.

In less than 2 years our Tuesday night Bible study grew from a group of 8 people to more than 300 people attending each Tuesday night. The Bible study then grew into a church. I was not the pastor of this church which soon grew to more than 1,000 people attending every Sunday morning. However, I did continue to teach the Tuesday night Bible study group for the next 10 years until I moved to Florida.

I do not share this testimony to glorify myself. I proved how unsuccessful I was by getting into severe financial problems. I give God all of the honor and glory for bringing me out of the ordeal that I faced. I thank Him for using a 2-year-old Christian to teach a Bible study that grew from 8 people every Tuesday night to a church with more than 1,000 people in attendance each Sunday morning.

I can tell you from the 12 years that I spent teaching that Bible study class and from the 24 books I have written (or co-authored with Judy) that *Scripture meditation works*. There is no question that Scripture meditation *will* work for you *if* you will faithfully obey your Father's instructions to allow your ears to hear your mouth boldly speaking His Word as you meditate day and night on the holy Scriptures.

I began my Scripture meditation by using 3x5 file cards. I had a thick pack of cards that I held together with a rubber band. This packet contained the Scripture verses that I meditated on during those difficult early months as a Christian when failure of our business seemed imminent.

I can remember having some of these cards taped to the walls of our home. I had them taped to the mirror in my bathroom. I carried them with me in my car when I drove. I used to boldly speak the Scripture I was meditating on while I drove the car.

I meditated continually on Scripture. I lived in a world of constant Scripture meditation. I immersed myself in God's Word. As the weeks turned into months and the months turned into years, our business turned around.

One way that you could begin your Scripture meditation is to build your own file of 3x5 Scripture cards. However, we have done a lot of this work for you. You might want to consider our Scripture Meditation cards. Judy and I have co-authored the following ten sets of Scripture Meditation Cards:

- *Receive Healing from the Lord*
- *Freedom from Worry and Fear*
- *Enjoy God's Wonderful Peace*
- *God Is Always with You*
- *Continually Increasing Faith in God*
- *Receive God's Blessings in Adversity*
- *Financial Instructions from God*
- *Find God's Will for Your Life*
- *A Closer Relationship with the Lord*
- *Our Father's Wonderful Love*

Each of these sets of Scripture cards contains 52 2-1/2" x 3-1/2" cards with Scripture for you to meditate on pertaining to the topic of that set of Scripture cards. Each set contains approximately 80 passages of Scripture because some of the cards contain more than one passage of Scripture.

If you are interested in any of these topics, we recommend the Scripture Meditation cards pertaining to that topic. Instead of having to build your own 3x5 cards, you will have 52 Scripture cards that already have been prepared for you.

Each set of Scripture cards is accompanied by a CD. On each CD I explain every verse of Scripture in that set of cards. This explanation will help your Scripture meditation. These Scripture cards and the CDs can be ordered with the order form in the back of this book or from our website – www.lamplight.net.

You also might want to look at the list of books that I have written or co-authored with Judy. These books are listed on the order form at the end of this book and also on our website.

Each of these books contains hundreds of verses of Scripture. I have devoted thousands of hours to writing these books. Even though I now am 80 years old, I still write every day. I know that I am doing what God has called me to do. I am very focused on completing the assignment that God has given to me.

In addition to the Scripture on the 10 sets of Scripture Meditation cards, you can build additional Scripture cards by going through these books. You can choose Scripture that you find in your own Bible study and put that Scripture on your own Scripture cards.

Absolutely refuse to focus on any problem you face. We are not saying that you should ignore the problem. Identify the problem. *Then* focus continually on appropriate promises from God's Word instead of focusing on the problem.

Meditate day and night on God's specific promises that you have chosen. Your ears should consistently hear your mouth boldly speaking promises from God. As you do this, God Himself will speak to you through the supernatural power of His living Word.

Treat every verse of Scripture that you are meditating on as a personal promise from your Father to you. Personalize the promise. Do not let up. Your Father instructs you to meditate day and night on His Word.

Get in there and fight in the spiritual realm. You fight spiritual battles *with your mouth*. You will receive constant encouragement from God if you faithfully obey His instructions to meditate day and night on whatever passages of Scripture you have chosen to meditate on.

Chapter 7

Fill Your Mind and Your Heart with the Word of God

You have learned the vital importance of renewing your mind daily in God's Word and meditating day and night on the holy Scriptures. Bible study and Scripture meditation are very important at every stage of your life, but obeying God's instructions in this area is especially important during the final years of your life.

When you consistently *study* the Word of God, you renew your *mind* with God's Word. When you *meditate* day and night on God's Word, the Scripture that you are meditating on will drop from your mind down into your *heart* after you have meditated on Scripture over a period of time. "...you shall lay up these My words in your [minds and] hearts and in your [entire] being..." (Deuteronomy 11:18 AMP)

If you have money in a savings account, a money market fund, a stock or any other form of investment, you are able to draw on this money when an emergency comes into your life. This same principle applies to storing up God's Word in your mind and your heart. The following words that King Solomon spoke to his son also are God's words to you. "...keep my words; lay up within you my commandments [for use when needed] and treasure them." (Proverbs 7:1 AMP)

Please note the words "for use when needed" in the amplification of this verse. God's Word is a spiritual treasure. The more of God's Word that you have stored up within yourself, the better off you will be when you face adversity.

As you grow older, you must not neglect your Father's specific instructions to consistently fill your eyes, your ears, your mind, your heart and your mouth with His supernatural Word. Your faith in God will be in direct proportion to the amount of God's Word that you have within yourself. "...The Word (God's message in Christ) is near you, on your lips and in your heart; that is, the Word (the message, the basis and object) of faith..." (Romans 10:8 AMP)

Please note the words "the basis and object of faith" in this verse and the amplification. The Word of God is the foundation for your faith in God. You should store up as much of this spiritual treasure within yourself as you possibly can during your final years on earth. "Receive, I pray you, the law and instruction from His mouth and lay up His words in your heart. If you return to the Almighty [and submit and humble yourself before Him], you will be built up..." (Job 22:22-23 AMP)

We often say that God emphasizes through repetition. You already have seen the words "lay up" repeated three times in this chapter. There is no doubt that your loving Father wants *you* to store up His Word in your mind and in your heart.

Your Father instructs you to "submit and humble yourself before Him." He wants you to have a deep and sincere desire to have *so much* of His Word inside of yourself that you will build yourself up spiritually. You should have such a solid spiritual foundation that you will be able to draw on this foundation at any time in your life, particularly as you grow older.

The home for your Bible is not on a desk, a table or a bookcase in your home. The Bible explains where the home of the Word of God should be. "Let the word [spoken by] Christ (the Messiah) have its home [in your hearts and minds] and dwell in you in [all its] richness..." (Colossians 3:16 AMP)

Some Christians give the Bible a place of honor in their homes. This is good, but you must realize that God has told you that the home for His Word should be in your heart and in your mind.

Your Father repeatedly emphasizes that He wants you to store up His Word in your mind and in your heart. You cannot spend your time more profitably during your final years on earth than to renew your mind in the Word of God each day and to meditate day and night on the holy Scriptures. Fill your mind and your heart continually with God's supernatural living Word. Jesus said, "…Your Word is Truth." (John 17:17 AMP)

The world is filled with the lies of Satan who is the impetus behind every lie. Jesus said, "…there is no truth in him. When he speaks a falsehood, he speaks what is natural to him, for he is a liar [himself] and the father of lies and of all that is false." (John 8:44 AMP)

In these last days before the return of Jesus Christ when Satan and his demons are so active in the world, your mind and your heart must be filled with Truth. The following words that Jesus spoke to His disciples apply to your life today. Jesus said, "…you will know the Truth, and the Truth will set you free." (John 8:32 AMP)

If your eyes, your ears, your mind, your heart and your mouth are filled to overflowing with the Truth of God's Word, you will be set free from being overcome by adversity during your final years on earth. You will be set free to the degree that you know what God's Word says, that you faithfully obey your Father's instructions and to the degree that you have deep, strong and unwavering faith in Him and in His promises. "…the Word of God is [always] abiding in you (in your hearts), and you have been victorious over the wicked one." (I John 2:14 AMP)

If your heart is filled with the Word of God, you will be able to walk in the victory that Jesus Christ won over Satan. Satan and his demons do everything they can to try to influence elderly people to be afraid and to believe untruths. Your best possible defense against Satan and his demons is a heart that is filled with the Word of God.

Do not allow negative thoughts and negative emotions to dominate your thinking during the final years of your life. "…the [uncompromisingly] righteous (the upright, in right standing with God) shall be in everlasting remembrance. He shall not be afraid of evil tidings; his heart is firmly fixed, trusting (leaning on and being confident) in the Lord. His heart is established and steady, he will not be afraid…" (Psalm 112:6-8 AMP)

When this verse and the amplification speak of the "uncompromisingly righteous" who are "in right standing with God," these words refer to every person who has received Jesus Christ as his or her Savior. If Jesus is your Savior, you *are* righteous before God. You are not righteous because of anything you have done, but because of the awesome price that Jesus paid to allow you to be righteous before God.

You are instructed to be "in everlasting remembrance" of God. Every aspect of your life should revolve around your heart and your mind being filled with God's Word as a result of studying the Bible each day and meditating day and night on the holy Scriptures.

The Word of God in your heart is a tremendous source of security at any time in your life, but a heart filled with God's Word is especially helpful during the final years of your life. If your heart is filled with God's Word, you will not be afraid of bad news. The good news of God's Word that fills your heart will enable you to cope with any bad news that you receive. Your heart will be firmly fixed because you trust completely in God and His Word.

If you have health challenges or any other challenges during the final years of your life, you must be able to draw on the Word of God that fills your heart. "…as he thinks in his heart, so is he…." (Proverbs 23:7 AMP)

You always will react to a crisis situation based on whatever you truly believe deep down in your heart where the hidden person of the heart lives. Jesus said, "…out of the fullness (the overflow, the superabundance) of the heart the mouth speaks. The good man from his inner good treasure flings forth good things, and the evil man out of his inner evil storehouse flings forth evil things." (Matthew 12:34-35 AMP)

What is your heart filled with? Is your heart filled with the Word of God? You will react to adversity at any time of your life, especially during your final years, by the words that you speak. If you have consistently stored up God's Word in your heart, your heart will overflow with God's Word. You will boldly speak the Word of God when you face adversity.

If you have not paid the price of filling your heart with God's Word, the words that come out of your mouth in a crisis can pull you down. Your words will not be able to compare with words that pour out of a heart that is filled to overflowing with the supernatural Word of God. "A glad heart makes a cheerful countenance, but by sorrow of heart the spirit is broken." (Proverbs 15:13 AMP)

You will have a glad heart if your heart is filled with God's Word. If you allow sorrow to become deeply rooted in your heart, your spirit will be broken. The sorrow in your heart will dominate your life. "All the days of the desponding and afflicted are made evil [by anxious thoughts and forebodings], but he who has a glad heart has a continual feast [regardless of circumstances]." (Proverbs 15:15 AMP)

Every day of your life can be made evil by the influence of Satan and his demons. If you allow this to happen, you will be worried and anxious about the future because you have not obeyed your Father's instructions to fill your heart with His Word.

If your heart is filled with God's Word, your heart will rejoice regardless of the problems you face. The supernatural power of God's Word in your heart will be much greater than the severity of any adversity you face. "Be happy [in your faith] and rejoice and be glad-hearted continually (always)" (I Thessalonians 5:16 AMP)

You should be happy at all times because of your deep, strong and unwavering faith in God and His Word. Your Father does not want your happiness to be determined by what does or does not happen in your life. If your heart is filled with God's Word, your faith in God will be anchored on a solid supernatural foundation. You will not give in to discouragement. God's Word that fills your heart will prevail over the severity of whatever problems you face.

This chapter has been devoted entirely to explaining what God's Word says about filling *your mind* and *your heart* with God's supernatural Word. In the next chapter you will learn that the Word of God actually is spiritual medicine that your Father has provided for you.

Chapter 8

God Has Provided You with Powerful Spiritual Medicine

Many older people face health challenges. They require prescription medicine to cope with these challenges. Your loving Father has provided you with the most effective medicine that has ever existed. "A happy heart is good medicine and a cheerful mind works healing, but a broken spirit dries up the bones." (Proverbs 17:22 AMP)

If your heart is filled with God's Word and you consistently meditate on what God has promised instead of dwelling on the problems you face, you will partake of the supernatural medicine that God has provided for you. You will have a happy heart. If you have renewed your mind daily in God's Word, you will have a cheerful mind. You will not have the broken spirit that some people have because their minds and their hearts are not filled with the Word of God. "He sends forth His word and heals them…" (Psalm 107:20 AMP)

The Word of God has supernatural healing power. You do not partake of God's medicine by swallowing a capsule or receiving an injection. You partake of God's supernatural medicine by faithfully obeying your Father's instructions to consistently fill your eyes, your ears, your mind, your heart and your mouth with the supernatural medicine of His Word. "The law of the Lord is perfect, restoring the [whole] person…" (Psalm 19:7 AMP)

Please note the words "restoring the whole person" in this verse and the amplification. These words include your body. Your body will be restored if you consistently partake of the medicine of God's Word.

The Great Physician has told you how often you should take His medicine. You saw in Joshua 1:8 and Psalm 1:2 that God instructs you to take His medicine *throughout the day and night*. God instructs you in II Corinthians 4:16 to take His medicine *day after day*. Ephesians 4:23 instructs you to take God's medicine *constantly*.

When a doctor gives you a prescription, you often are limited as to the amount of medicine you can take because an overdose could harm you. The Great Physician does not limit His medicine. You cannot overdose on God's medicine. You can take as much of God's medicine as you desire at any time during every day and night of your life.

The Word of God is multi-faceted. In addition to being God's medicine, God's Word also is a spiritual seed. Jesus said, "…The seed is the Word of God." (Luke 8:11 AMP)

Jesus spoke these words as part of a parable that explained God's laws of sowing and reaping. You should plant the spiritual seed of God's Word in the spiritual soil that God has provided. Your mind is spiritual soil. You plant seeds in this spiritual soil if you faithfully obey God's instructions to continually renew your mind in His Word. Your heart is spiritual soil. You will plant the seed of God's Word in your heart if you faithfully obey God's instructions to meditate day and night on His Word.

If you consistently speak words of worry, fear, doubt or unbelief that are caused by focusing on adversity, these negative words will plant negative seeds in your mind and in your heart. Seeds have great multiplying power. In the natural realm a small seed is able to multiply itself many times over to produce a harvest. This same principle applies in the spiritual realm.

This book is filled with hundreds of spiritual seeds that will help you to obey your Father's instructions pertaining to growing older. If you faithfully obey God's instructions about planting these seeds, your Father will give you a bountiful harvest.

We have explained that the Word of God is multi-faceted. The Word of God is God's medicine. The Word of God is a spiritual seed. The Word of God also is spiritual food that your Father has provided for you. When Job faced severe adversity he said, "...I have esteemed and treasured the words of His mouth more than my necessary food." (Job 23:12 AMP)

You should feed your body with wholesome food to be healthy (see Chapter 24). The food of God's Word is even *more* important than the "necessary food" that you feed your body.

You should nourish your mind and your heart every day and night with the spiritual food of God's Word. You should be like the prophet Jeremiah who said, "Your words were found, and I ate them; and Your words were to me a joy and the rejoicing of my heart..." (Jeremiah 15:16 AMP)

If you constantly eat the spiritual food that God has provided for you, your heart will sing with joy. Unfortunately, many Christians do not consistently feed their minds and their hearts with spiritual food. Jesus said, "...It has been written, Man shall not live and be upheld and sustained by bread alone, but by every word that comes forth from the mouth of God." (Matthew 4:4 AMP)

You need much more than wholesome and nutritious food for your body. You must understand the importance of consistently partaking of the spiritual nourishment your Father has provided. The apostle Paul told Timothy that he should be "...ever nourishing your own self on the truths of the faith..." (I Timothy 4:6 AMP)

Please note the words "ever nourishing" in this verse. You should nourish yourself continually with the supernatural food of God's Word. You *eat* spiritual food by studying the Word of God as you consistently renew your mind in God's Word. You *digest* your spiritual food by meditating day and night on the Word of God.

In the natural realm, the food that you eat, digest and assimilate is converted into physical energy. This same principle applies in the spiritual realm.

In the world, some people limit the amount of food that they eat because they do not want to gain weight. God does not place any limit on the amount of spiritual food that you can feed yourself. Your Father wants you to *feast* day and night on the supernatural food that He has provided. "Anxiety in a man's heart weighs it down, but an encouraging word makes it glad." (Proverbs 12:25 AMP)

If you allow worry, anxiety, dread and fear to get into your heart, you will be heavy-hearted. If you consistently fill your heart with God's Word, you will have a glad heart that sings with joy.

This verse speaks of "an encouraging word." Think about the meaning of the words "discourage" and "encourage." The prefix "dis" in the word discourage means "lack of." The prefix "en" in the word encourage means "in." Instead of allowing any adversity that you face to take courage *out* of you, you should consistently put courage *into* yourself by meditating day and night on God's Word. The apostle Paul said, "...whatever was thus written in former days was written for our instruction, that by [our steadfast and patient] endurance and the encouragement [drawn] from the Scriptures we might hold fast to and cherish hope." (Romans 15:4 AMP)

God anointed human authors many years ago to write inspired words in the Bible for your instruction. The Word of God in your heart will enable you to endure when you face adversity. Once again you are told that you will be *encouraged* by God's Word. You put courage into yourself when you consistently study and meditate on the Word of God. You will not give up hope if you constantly fill your mind and your heart with encouragement from the holy Scriptures.

When David faced severe problems, he asked God to strengthen him with the promises in His Word. David prayed to God saying, "My life dissolves and weeps itself away for heaviness; raise me up and strengthen me according to [the promises of] Your word." (Psalm 119:28 AMP)

God answered this prayer. Shortly after David prayed, the Bible explains that David was strengthened as he studied and meditated on the Word of God. David said, "This is my comfort and consolation in my affliction: that Your word has revived me and given me life." (Psalm 119:50 AMP)

Your Father wants to comfort you and encourage you when you face adversity. His supernatural living Word will encourage you as you grow older.

Many older people face significant problems because of pain and discomfort in their bodies. One of the best things that you can do if you are experiencing pain and discomfort is to encourage yourself by meditating day and night on God's supernatural living Word. If there ever was a time when you should increase your Scripture meditation, your final years on earth are that time. Instead of allowing yourself to be discouraged by health challenges or by any other challenges you face, you will be encouraged if you consistently fill your mind and your heart with the Word of God.

This chapter contains many interesting verses of Scripture pertaining to God's medicine, spiritual seeds and spiritual food. You have seen that you will be encouraged and strengthened if you consistently fill your mind and your heart with God's Word. In the next chapter we will study the Bible to learn how you can experience the supernatural peace of God throughout the final years of your life, regardless of the circumstances you face.

Chapter 9

Focus Continually on God and His Word

As you grow older, you may face challenges with your health or other challenges that are very severe. No matter what you face, you should react to severe problems the way that King Jehoshaphat reacted when he faced a hostile army that was much too powerful for him and his army to overcome. He said, "...we have no might to stand against this great company that is coming against us. We do not know what to do, but our eyes are upon You." (II Chronicles 20:12 AMP)

King Jehoshaphat admitted that there was no way his army could prevail against their much stronger opponent. He admitted that he did not know what to do. Then he said the words that apply to *you* whenever you face difficult problems. King Jehoshaphat said, "Our eyes are upon You."

Your Father repeatedly instructs you to focus on Him and the supernatural promises in His Word instead of focusing on whatever problems you face. We are not saying that you should ignore difficult problems. King Jehoshaphat did not ignore the problem. He admitted the severity of the problem that he faced. He then turned *away* from this problem to focus on God. Your Father wants you to do the same. "Hear, my son, and be wise, and direct your mind in the way [of the Lord]." (Proverbs 23:19 AMP)

If you are spiritually wise and mature, you will direct your mind to focus continually on the Lord. Your loving Father has instructed you to "...lead every thought and purpose away captive into the obedience of Christ (the Messiah, the Anointed One)" (II Corinthians 10:5 AMP)

Please note the word "every" in this verse. You are instructed to direct *all* of your thoughts away from whatever problem you face. You are instructed to bring "every thought and purpose captive into the obedience of Christ." Focus on Jesus instead of focusing on any pain and discomfort in your body or any other problem you face as you grow older.

Whatever you focus on is magnified. The prefix "magni" means big or large. When something is magnified, it is made larger. If you magnify any problem that you face, you make the problem seem like a "big problem." You make God seem like "little God."

He is "big, big God." Your problems are "little problems" compared to the supernatural omnipotence of God. "…You have made the heavens and the earth by Your great power and by Your outstretched arm! There is nothing too hard or too wonderful for You" (Jeremiah 32:17 AMP)

The same God Who created heaven and earth with His great power is ready, willing and able to help you (see Psalm 21:2, Isaiah 41:13 and Hebrews 4:16 and 13:6). No problems are too difficult for God to solve.

God is Almighty God, not "part-mighty" God. He is omnipotent. His power is unlimited. God will help you with every problem you face if you will turn to Him with deep, strong and unwavering faith in Him instead of magnifying any problem that you face.

This book is filled with hundreds of verses of Scripture that will strengthen and encourage you when you face adversity. Our ten sets of Scripture Meditation cards, all of the other books we have written and your own Bible are filled with many additional promises from God.

You saw in Chapter 5 that God instructs you to meditate day and night on His Word. Your mind cannot think of two things at the same time. If you truly are meditating day and night on God's

Word, there is no way that any problem you face can gain a place of ascendancy in your mind. "...Do not be afraid of the enemy; [earnestly] remember the Lord and imprint Him [on your minds]..." (Nehemiah 4:14 AMP)

This verse and the amplification instruct you to "earnestly remember the Lord." When you do something earnestly, you do whatever you are doing wholeheartedly. You are instructed to *imprint* God on your mind. If you obey this instruction, your mind will be so focused on God and His Word that any problem you face will not be able to obtain a foothold in your mind.

Your Father wants you to be single-minded, not double-minded. He does not want your mind to go back and forth from faith in Him to worrying about whatever problem you face. "Turn not aside to the right hand or to the left; remove your foot from evil." (Proverbs 4:27 AMP)

This passage of Scripture instructs you to keep looking straight ahead. Do not turn to the right. Do not turn to the left. Keep moving forward, focusing on God by meditating day and night on His Word as He has instructed you to do. Immerse yourself in God's Word. The evil of Satan will not influence you if you obey this instruction.

Jesus faced many severe problems during His earthly ministry. He absolutely refused to take His focus away from His Father and His unwavering faith in Him.

The following verse of Scripture consists of prophetic words that Isaiah spoke regarding Jesus Christ. "For the Lord God helps Me; therefore have I not been ashamed *or* confounded. Therefore have I set My face like a flint, and I know that I shall not be put to shame." (Isaiah 50:7 AMP)

Apply these words to whatever challenge you face. Jesus was certain that God would help Him. He was not concerned about any adversity He faced. He was single-minded at all times.

When Jesus spoke of "setting His face like a flint," He referred to unwavering faith. A flint is a very hard and unyielding rock. Your Father wants your faith in Him to be unyielding and unwavering because you are absolutely certain that He *will* bring you safely through whatever ordeal you face according to your faith in Him. "...he who has My word, let him speak My word faithfully...." (Jeremiah 23:28 AMP)

You will speak God's Word faithfully if you obey your Father's instructions to meditate day and night on His Word. *Your* ears should hear *your* mouth consistently saying what God says instead of talking about whatever problem you face. Focus continually on God. "You will guard him and keep him in perfect and constant peace whose mind [both its inclination and its character] is stayed on You, because he commits himself to You, leans on You, and hopes confidently in You." (Isaiah 26:3 AMP)

Your loving Father promises that *He* will "guard *you* and keep *you* in perfect and constant peace." What does God require you to do to receive manifestation of this magnificent promise in your life? Your Father instructs you to keep your mind *stayed* on Him. He instructs you to focus continually on Him because you trust Him totally, completely and absolutely. You should be like the psalmist who said, "Great peace have they who love Your law..." (Psalm 119:165 AMP)

How do you receive God's supernatural peace? You will receive manifestation of His supernatural peace if you *love His Word*. If you love God's Word, you *will* meditate on it day and night as your Father has instructed you to do. You will keep God and His Word at the forefront of your consciousness at all times.

You will be like the psalmist David who said, "I have set the Lord continually before me; because He is at my right hand, I shall not be moved. Therefore my heart is glad and my glory [my inner self] rejoices; my body too shall rest and confidently dwell in safety." (Psalm 16:8-9 AMP)

If you focus *continually* on the Lord, you will *not* be moved by the seeming severity of any problem you face. Your heart will sing with joy because of your absolute certainty that God will bring you safely through all adversity just as His Word repeatedly says that He will. "...he who has once entered [God's] rest also has ceased from [the weariness and pain] of human labors..." (Hebrews 4:10 AMP)

David rested in God because he focused continually on God. Your Father wants *you* to rest in Him. He does not want you to be afraid because you know that any problem you face is too difficult to solve with your human abilities. You are instructed to *"cease from the weariness and pain of human labors."*

The Greek philosopher Plato once said, "When physical eyesight declines, spiritual eyesight increases." You must continue to grow spiritually throughout the final years of your life. "...learn to sense what is vital, and approve and prize what is excellent and of real value..." (Philippians 1:10 AMP)

Focusing on the ways of God instead of focusing on anything in the world is *vital*. Do not allow anything in the world to distract you from focusing continually on God.

In the final chapters of this book we will share with you many things that we have learned regarding physical fitness. We are *not* trying to de-emphasize the importance of physical fitness. However, the following passage of Scripture compares physical fitness to spiritual fitness. "...Train yourself toward godliness (piety), [keeping yourself spiritually fit]. For physical training is of some value (useful for a little), but godliness (spiritual training) is useful and of value in everything and in every way, for it holds promise for the present life and also for the life which is to come." (I Timothy 4:7-8 AMP)

The amplification of verse 7 instructs you to "keep yourself spiritually fit." If you faithfully obey God's instructions to meditate day and night on His Word, you will grow and mature spiritually throughout the final years of your life. You will be blessed during the remainder of your life on earth and also when you are in heaven. "...let us go on and get past the elementary stage in the teachings and doctrine of Christ (the Messiah), advancing steadily toward the completeness and perfection that belong to spiritual maturity...." (Hebrews 6:1 AMP)

Refuse to stay in spiritual kindergarten. You are instructed to "go on and get past elementary teaching." Your Father wants you to advance steadily toward spiritual maturity. As you grow older, you should consistently learn more eternal truths from God's Word.

You never stand still in the spiritual realm. If you are not moving forward, you are moving backward. Jesus said, "…whoever has [spiritual knowledge], to him will more be given and he will be furnished richly so that he will have abundance; but from him who has not, even what he has will be taken away." (Matthew 13:12 AMP)

If you do not consistently grow and mature spiritually, the spiritual knowledge that you have will depart. *You decide.* Will you steadily move forward in spiritual maturity during the final years of your life? Will you turn away from the superficial ways of the world to continually turn toward God? Your Father has given you a marvelous opportunity to learn great spiritual truths. Do not waste the opportunity that has been given to you.

The final years of your life should be a time of spiritual growth. As you grow older, you should become more flexible instead of becoming inflexible as some older people do. Do not allow your thinking to become rigid.

If you will pay the price to learn and consistently obey the scriptural instructions that we are sharing with you, you will be excited about everything you are learning from God's Word. You will be ecstatic as you grow older because you will be living your life the way your Father has instructed you to live.

Chapter 10

Your Life Belongs to Jesus Christ

If Jesus Christ is your Savior, your life belongs to Him, *not* to you. Jesus paid a tremendous price for you. "…He died for all, so that all those who live might live no longer to and for themselves, but to and for Him Who died and was raised again for their sake." (II Corinthians 5:15 AMP)

The word "all" is used twice in the first seven words of this verse. This word includes you. Jesus died for you so that you would no longer live for yourself. Jesus was raised again from death for you. "…You are not your own, you were bought with a price [purchased with a preciousness and paid for, made His own]. So then, honor God and bring glory to Him in your body." (I Corinthians 6:19-20 AMP)

God often emphasizes through repetition. You have just seen two passages of Scripture telling you that your life does not belong to you because of the price that Jesus paid for you.

Your loving Father will bless you abundantly *if* you live your life in obedience to these instructions. "…whoever looks intently into the perfect law that gives freedom, and continues in it – not forgetting what they have heard, but doing it – they will be blessed in what they do." (James 1:25 NIV)

You are instructed to look intently into God's Word as you renew your mind each day and meditate day and night on the Word of God. God promises that you will receive freedom and other blessings from Him if you faithfully obey His instructions.

You have learned that God has promised to carry you from the time you are born throughout your old age (see Isaiah 46:3-4). God can do whatever He desires, but He often will carry you only to the degree that you will submit your life to Him by obeying His instructions. "Blessed (happy, fortunate, to be envied) are they who keep His testimonies, and who seek, inquire for and of Him and crave Him with the whole heart." (Psalm 119:2 AMP)

Your Father promises to bless you abundantly *if* you do what He instructs you to do. He will bless you if you seek Him with all your heart.

You have learned that the Word of God will fill your *mind* when you obey God's instructions to renew your mind in His Word each day. You have learned that God's Word will fill your *heart* and your *mouth* if you faithfully obey your Father's instructions to meditate day and night on His Word. "…the word is very near you, in your mouth and in your mind and in your heart, so that you can do it." (Deuteronomy 30:14 AMP)

Why should you fill your mind, your heart and your mouth with the supernatural Word of God? The answer to this question is so that you will *do* what your Father instructs you to do. Studying and meditating on God's Word is only the beginning. You must *obey* what you have learned from God by studying and meditating on His Word.

Many people face significant challenges during the final years of their lives. These people must learn and obey God's instructions. "…the Lord shall make you the head, and not the tail; and you shall be above only, and you shall not be beneath, if you heed the commandments of the Lord your God which I command you this day and are watchful to do them." (Deuteronomy 28:13 AMP)

Personalize this promise. Meditate on it. Open your mouth and state that you will not be overcome by any problem you face. Boldly say that you are "the head and not the tail" and that you are above whatever problem you face, not beneath.

This promise is conditional. You will overcome *if* you consistently learn and obey God's instructions. God commands you to do what He has instructed you to do. The psalmist understood this principle when he said, "Streams of water run down my eyes, because men do not keep Your law [they hear it not, nor receive it, love it, or obey it]." (Psalm 119:136 AMP)

The psalmist actually cried when he observed people who did not love, receive and obey God's Word. Your Father wants you to be humble and teachable. He has given you specific instructions telling you exactly how to live throughout the final years of your life.

You should be open to learn and to obey *everything* that your Father has instructed you to do so that you will come safely through your final years as your loving Father very much wants you to do. "…Blessed (happy, fortunate, to be envied) is the man who fears (reveres and worships) the Lord, who delights greatly in His commandments." (Psalm 112:1 AMP)

Fear God and revere Him. Every aspect of your life should revolve around your absolute awe of and reverence for God. Delight in God's Word. Hunger for the magnificent supernatural food that your Father has provided for you. "The secret [of the sweet, satisfying companionship] of the Lord have they who fear (revere and worship) Him…" (Psalm 25:14 AMP)

This verse explains the secret of a close and intimate relationship with God. *If* you truly fear God and revere Him and hold Him in constant awe, you will focus continually on Him during the final years of your life. You will do your very best to live your life in complete obedience to the instructions your Father has given to you.

Does every aspect of your life revolve around your deep and constant gratitude toward Jesus Christ for the enormous price that He paid for your sins? "…so that He alone in everything and in every respect might occupy the chief place [stand first and be preeminent]." (Colossians 1:18 AMP)

You are instructed to put Jesus in first place in every area of your life. The amplification says that Jesus should be preeminent in your life. Do not allow anyone or anything to come ahead of Jesus. He has earned and He deserves the right to be in first place in your life at all times. John the Baptist said, "He must increase, but I must decrease. [He must grow more prominent; I must grow less so.]" (John 3:30 AMP)

As you grow and mature as a Christian, you should do what the amplification in this verse instructs you to do. Jesus Christ "must grow more prominent" in your life. The pursuit of your personal desires "must grow less so." You are headed for inevitable problems if you insist on doing what you want to do. Put Jesus in first place, other people in second place and yourself in last place (see Philippians 2:3-5).

Live the final years of your life by humbling yourself more and more before Jesus and before others. Do not block God from blessing you the way that He wants to bless you by insisting on living your life the way that you want to live.

If you have been a Christian for many years, you should have grown and matured spiritually. "Who is wise and understanding among you? Let them show it by their good life, by deeds done in the humility that comes from wisdom." (James 3:13 NIV)

You will live a humble life if you learn and understand God's instructions. A proud life comes from lack of spiritual maturity. "He leads the humble in what is right, and the humble He teaches His way." (Psalm 25:9 AMP)

Your Father will lead you if you are humble. He teaches His children who are humble and teachable. "…He gives His undeserved favor to the low [in rank], the humble, and the afflicted." (Proverbs 3:34 AMP)

God will give His undeserved and unearned grace to you if you truly are humble. Devote your life to living the way that God instructs you to live. "…turn not aside from following the Lord, but serve Him with all your heart. And turn not aside after vain and worthless things which cannot profit or deliver you, for they are empty and futile." (I Samuel 12:20-21 AMP)

This passage of Scripture emphasizes the vital importance of following God and serving Him wholeheartedly. Do not make the mistake that some older people make of pursuing worldly goals that are "empty and futile" from God's perspective.

Turn away from the superficial ways of the world. Turn away from selfish goals. A self-centered life always will bring problems into your life. The only question is when, not if.

Many older people waste their final years on earth. They focus on earthly things that have no eternal significance. They block God from carrying them every step of the way throughout the final years of their lives as He has promised to do.

In this chapter you have learned that your life belongs to Jesus Christ. You have learned the vital importance of fearing God, of obeying God's instructions and of keeping God in first place at all times. The Scripture references in the next chapter will explain how to achieve these important goals.

Chapter 11

God Lives in Your Heart

If you keep God in first place at all times, the final years of your life will be meaningful, productive and fulfilling. Your life should revolve around your continuing consciousness of the magnificent indwelling presence of God. "One God and Father of [us] all, Who is above all [Sovereign over all], pervading all and [living] in [us] all." (Ephesians 4:6 AMP)

The word "all" is used five times in this one short verse of Scripture and the amplification. You are told that God is "above all, pervading all and living in us all." If Jesus Christ is your Savior, the same God Who created you *lives in your heart*. You are never alone. Your loving Father is with you throughout every minute of every hour of every day of your life.

God is omnipresent. God is *not* limited to sitting on His throne in heaven. He is able to be in an infinite number of places at the same time. The same God Who sits on His throne in heaven is able to pervade the entire world. The word "pervade" means to be spread out. God is spread out all over the world. He lives in the heart of *every* person who has received Jesus Christ as his or her Savior.

Jesus Christ Who died for you on the cross at Calvary *also* lives in your heart. As you grow and mature as a Christian, you will become increasingly certain that Jesus *really does* live in your heart. "...Do you not yourselves realize and know [thoroughly by an ever-increasing experience] that Jesus Christ is in you?" (II Corinthians 13:5 AMP)

Jesus is omnipresent just as God is omnipresent. Jesus is able to be in an infinite number of places at the same time. The Bible teaches that Jesus sits at the right hand of His Father in heaven (see Mark 16:11, Ephesians 1:20 and Colossians 3:11). Jesus is not limited to being in heaven. He can and does live in the heart of every person throughout the world who has received Him as his or her Savior.

The apostle Paul was very conscious of this great spiritual truth. Paul said, "I have been crucified with Christ [in Him I have shared His crucifixion]; it is no longer I who live, but Christ (the Messiah) lives in me; and the life I now live in the body I live by faith in (by adherence to and reliance on and complete trust in) the Son of God, Who loved me and gave Himself up for me." (Galatians 2:20 AMP)

The amplification of this verse says that Paul "shared the crucifixion" of Jesus Christ. Paul *died* to his selfish desires just as Jesus died for the sins of every person in the world. Jesus gave up everything. Paul gave up everything.

Paul said that he no longer deserved to control his life because Jesus lived in his heart. Paul continually surrendered control and placed absolute trust in Jesus Who lived in him.

If Jesus Christ is your Savior, your life is not your own. *Die* to Christ. *Surrender* your life to Him. Trust Him completely. As you go through the final years of your life, make the quality decision to allow Jesus to be in complete control. He has more than earned the right to control your life.

You have seen that God the Father lives in your heart. You have seen that Jesus Christ lives in your heart. The Bible also teaches that the Holy Spirit lives in the heart of every person who has received Jesus Christ as his or her Savior. "Do you not know that your body is the temple (the very sanctuary) of the Holy Spirit Who lives within you, Whom you have received [as a Gift] from God?..." (I Corinthians 6:19 AMP)

Your body is the temple of the Holy Spirit. The Greek word "naos" that is translated as "temple" in this verse actually means a shrine. A shrine in this context is a hallowed and sacred place. You should be in absolute awe that the Holy Spirit lives in your heart. This verse and the amplification say that the Holy Spirit is a precious Gift that has been given to you by God.

If you understand the immensity of the truth that God the Father, Jesus Christ and the Holy Spirit *all* live in *your* heart, you will be able to live the final years of your life with a continual consciousness of Who lives within you. "…in Him the whole fullness of Deity (the Godhead) continues to dwell in bodily form [giving complete expression of the divine nature]. And you are in Him, made full and having come to fullness of life [in Christ you too are filled with the Godhead – Father, Son and Holy Spirit – and reach full spiritual stature].…" (Colossians 2:9-10 AMP)

The word "Godhead" in the amplification refers to the Father, Son and Holy Spirit. If Jesus Christ is your Savior, "you are filled with the Godhead." God the Father, Jesus Christ and the Holy Spirit live inside of *you*.

You are a spiritual powerhouse. Almighty God lives in your heart. Jesus Christ lives in your heart. The Holy Spirit lives in your heart. You have inside of yourself supernatural spiritual power that is much greater and much more powerful than nuclear power or any other power on earth.

You have just seen that the Bible teaches that God lives *in* you. The Bible also teaches that God is *with* you at all times. "Have not I commanded you? Be strong, vigorous, and very courageous. Be not afraid, neither be dismayed, for the Lord your God is with you wherever you go." (Joshua 1:9 AMP)

These words that God spoke to Joshua when he succeeded Moses as the leader of the Israelites also apply to *you* throughout your life and especially during the final years of your life. God *commands* you to be strong and courageous. You will never be afraid if you are absolutely certain that God is with you at all times.

God does not play favorites (see Acts 10:34). If God was with Joshua throughout his life, you can be certain that He is with you throughout your life, if Jesus Christ is your Savior. This great truth is vitally important during the final years of your life. God said, "Fear not [there is nothing to fear], for I am with you; do not look around you in terror and be dismayed, for I am your God. I will strengthen and harden you to difficulties, yes, I will help you; yes, I will hold you up and retain you with My [victorious] right hand of rightness and justice." (Isaiah 41:10 AMP)

Why would you ever be afraid of *anything* if you are *absolutely certain* that God is with you at all times. If you are facing a difficult problem during the final years of your life, meditate day and night on your Father's promise to "strengthen you, to harden you to difficulties, to help you and to hold you up." Do not allow fatigue, sickness or anything else to draw you away from your absolute certainty that God is with you at all times and that He will strengthen you and help you.

The promises that we are studying about God being with you should be especially encouraging during the final years of your life. If you are facing a difficult challenge with your health, focus continually on God being in you and with you at all times instead of focusing on the pain and discomfort in your body.

If you are facing adversity, meditate day and night on these verses of Scripture that assure you that God, Jesus and the Holy Spirit live in your heart and that They are with you at all times. "…with us is the Lord our God to help us and to fight our battles…" (II Chronicles 32:8 AMP)

Do not allow yourself to be overcome by the seeming severity of any problem you face. You have just seen that your Father promises to help you. This verse tells you that He will fight your battles for you. Let go. Get out of the way. Have absolute faith that God will fight your battles for you just as He has promised to do. "…He [God] Himself has said, I will not in any way fail you nor give you up nor leave you without support. [I will] not, [I will] not, [I will] not in any degree leave you helpless nor forsake nor let [you] down (relax My hold on you)! [Assuredly not!]" (Hebrews 13:5 AMP)

Please note that this verse and the amplification use the words "I will not" three times. Your Father assures you that He will *not* leave you or forsake you. Are you facing adversity? Meditate continually on these magnificent promises that guarantee that God is with you, that He is watching over you and that He will never let you down. Every aspect of your life should revolve around your continual consciousness of God's indwelling presence. "…He is not far from each one of us. For in Him we live and move and have our being…" (Acts 17:27-28 AMP)

God is not a distant far away God. He could not be closer. You have seen that God lives in you. You have seen that He is with you at all times. You should "live and move and have your being" in your continual consciousness that God lives in you and that He is with you at all times. You should be like the psalmist who said, "My whole being follows hard after You and clings closely to You; Your right hand upholds me." (Psalm 63:8 AMP)

The psalmist was totally committed to God. He clung to God. He was certain that God would hold him up. This same assurance is available to you. Do not ever, and particularly during the final years of your life, think that you have to do everything apart from God. "…you must abide in (live in, never depart from) Him [being rooted in Him, knit to Him], just as [His anointing] has taught you [to do]." (I John 2:27 AMP)

This verse says that you must abide in God. Every aspect of your life should revolve around His indwelling presence. He will anoint you and guide you if your life truly does revolve around Him and if you trust Him completely. "The eternal God is your refuge and dwelling place, and underneath are the everlasting arms…" (Deuteronomy 33:27 AMP)

You saw in Chapter 1 that Isaiah 46:3-4 promises that God will carry you from the time you are born to the time that your hair is white with age. Your Father will hold you up with His everlasting arms. He will not let you down. God is your refuge. He is your dwelling place.

Your relationship with God should be deeper than just going to church once or twice each week and spending a few minutes each day in prayer. Your relationship with God should be close and intimate throughout every hour of every day of your life.

Chapter 12

Quiet and Confident Trust in God

Now that you have learned many great scriptural truths pertaining to the indwelling presence of God, we are ready to look into God's Word for specific instructions pertaining to a close and intimate relationship with God. As you grow older, you must understand the vital importance of continually drawing closer to God. If Jesus Christ is your Savior, you have been given the opportunity to enjoy an intimate relationship with God. "…in Christ Jesus you who once were far away have been brought near by the blood of Christ." (Ephesians 2:13 NIV)

Every person who has not received Jesus Christ as his or her Savior is far away from God. Every person on earth was born with a sin nature (see Romans 3:23). When you repent of your sins and ask God's forgiveness and trust Jesus Christ completely for eternal salvation, your sins are forgiven. You then are at peace with God. You are brought near to God.

Food is a necessity. You will starve if you go indefinitely without food. An intimate relationship with God is even more of a necessity than the food that you must have to sustain your body. God said, "…Seek Me [inquire for and of Me and require Me as you require food] and you shall live!" (Amos 5:4 AMP)

The word "require" is used twice in the amplification of this verse. When you require something, whatever you require is an absolute necessity. God instructs you to seek an intimate relationship with Him with the understanding that you require this close relationship in the spiritual realm just as you require food in the natural realm.

This book is filled with specific instructions from God that you should obey as you grow older. If you learn and obey these instructions, you will continually draw closer to God. "…this is how we may discern [daily, by experience] that we are coming to know Him [to perceive, recognize, understand, and become better acquainted with Him]: if we keep (bear in mind, observe, practice) His teachings (precepts, commandments)." (I John 2:3 AMP)

The amplification of this verse explains that the intimacy of your relationship with God should be a vital part of your everyday life. How do you draw closer to God? You will draw closer to God if you consistently obey His instructions. "Come close to God and He will come close to you…." (James 4:8 AMP)

You decide how close your relationship with God will be. This verse assures you that God *will* come close to you. However, you must initiate this relationship. You must have a deep and sincere desire to come close to God. *Are you* doing your very best to draw close to God?

As you grow older, you should not allow anything to come ahead of your strong desire to continually draw closer to God. You must have a close relationship with God to deal successfully with the challenges that many people face during the final years of their lives. If there ever was a time in your life to draw closer to God, the time immediately preceding the time that you die and go to be with Him in heaven is that time.

If you are close to God, you will not be worried about any problem you face. Your Father wants you to be quiet, calm and confident, regardless of the circumstances you face. "…a gentle and peaceful spirit, which [is not anxious or wrought up, but] is very precious in the sight of God." (I Peter 3:4 AMP)

The amplification of this verse says that God does not want you to be worried or anxious about anything. Your Father wants you to have "a gentle and peaceful spirit" at all times. This attitude is very important to God. "…the effect of righteousness will be peace [internal and external], and the result of righteousness will be quietness and confident trust forever." (Isaiah 32:17 AMP)

You become righteous before God when you receive Jesus Christ as your Savior. He is the Righteous One. You will live a righteous life if you consistently learn and obey the specific instructions that God has given to you in His Word.

If you live the way your Father instructs you to live, you will experience His supernatural peace in your life. You will be calm, quiet and confident at all times, regardless of the circumstances you face.

The Bible teaches that a definite relationship exists between being quiet, calm and confident and your physical health. "A calm and undisturbed mind and heart are the life and health of the body..." (Proverbs 14:30 AMP)

A "calm and undisturbed mind and heart" are vitally important as you grow older. This verse explains the relationship that exists between being quiet, calm and confident and your physical health.

Your Father will teach you through His Book of Instructions, the Bible, exactly what to do to remain calm when you face adversity. "Blessed (happy, fortunate, to be envied) is the man whom You discipline and instruct, O Lord, and teach out of Your law, that You may give him power to keep himself calm in the days of adversity..." (Psalm 94:12-13 AMP)

Your Father will bless you abundantly if you consistently allow Him to teach you out of His Word. He will show you exactly what to do so that you will be calm when you face adversity. This chapter is filled with similar instructions from God. If you obey God's instructions, you will be like the apostle Paul who said, "...I have learned how to be content (satisfied to the point where I am not disturbed or disquieted) in whatever state I am." (Philippians 4:11 AMP)

Paul was not always calm, quiet and confident regardless of the circumstances he faced. He said that he *learned* how to be quiet and calm and not to be upset regardless of the circumstances he faced. If Paul learned how to be calm, quiet and confident in the face of adversity, you also can learn this important spiritual lesson.

In Chapter 2 we studied the vital importance of renewing your mind in God's Word as you grow older. You can offset decay in your body by renewing your mind each day in the Word of God. You also learned in Chapter 5 that your Father instructs you to meditate day and night on His Word. If you have paid the price of consistently learning from God's Word, you will be calm, quiet and confident, regardless of the circumstances you face. "...a man of understanding has a cool spirit." (Proverbs 17:27 AMP)

If you turn away from the ways of the world because you understand God's ways (see Isaiah 55:8-9), you will have "a cool spirit." You will be calm, cool and collected deep down inside of yourself where the hidden person of your heart (the real you) lives (see I Peter 3:4). "Be still and rest in the Lord; wait for Him and patiently lean yourself upon Him..." (Psalm 37:7 AMP)

Your Father instructs you to be still at all times. You should rest in God and wait quietly and patiently for Him to bring you safely through whatever adversity you face. Do not allow yourself to become apprehensive and impatient if everything is not going the way that you desire. Lean on God. Trust Him completely. Trust God's timing just as you trust Him in every other area. Your Father has instructed you to "...be still, and know (recognize and understand) that I am God...." (Psalm 46:10 AMP)

Why does your Father instruct you to be still? He instructs you to be still because you *know* that He is God. He tells you to be still because you have total, complete and absolute faith in Him at all times, regardless of what is happening in your life.

The apostle Paul was a mentor to Timothy. Paul experienced a great deal of adversity in his life. The following advice that Paul gave to Timothy will help you as you grow older and face adversity in your life. Paul said, "...be calm and cool and steady, accept and suffer unflinchingly every hardship..." (II Timothy 4:5 AMP)

These anointed words that Paul spoke to Timothy also are God's specific instructions to you. Your Father instructs you to "be calm and cool and steady" at all times. Do not flinch when you face adversity. When someone flinches, that person draws back.

Calmly face up to all adversity because you are absolutely certain that God is always with you and that He will help you if you place all of your trust and confidence in Him (see Isaiah 41:13 and Hebrews 13:6). "...in quietness and in [trusting] confidence shall be your strength...." (Isaiah 30:15 AMP)

Your Father will strengthen you if you are quiet and confident because of your absolute trust in Him. Tension in the face of adversity blocks the power of God. Quiet confidence releases the strength of God into your life. *You decide* whether you will receive strength from God by whether or not you have paid the price to learn and obey these instructions from God pertaining to quietness and confidence.

Some people are born with a calm nature. Other people are relatively high strung from birth. Nevertheless, every Christian can learn how to be calm, quiet and confident in God Who is the source of true calmness.

Some people take tranquilizers because they are worried and anxious. Many older people who take tranquilizers are headed for problems. The only question is when, not if.

God is your tranquilizer. If Jesus Christ is your Savior, you can be certain that God lives in your heart. God is with you throughout every minute of every hour of every day of your life. If your life revolves around your certainty of His indwelling presence, you will not be worried and anxious. You will remain calm in the face of adversity.

Tension blocks faith in God. Your faith in God cannot operate effectively if you are tense. Your faith in God can only operate effectively to the degree that you are quiet and calm because you trust God completely to do what you cannot do yourself.

You have learned that God will keep you in perfect and constant peace if your mind is continually focused on Him (see Isaiah

26:3). If you obey God's instructions to renew your mind in His Word every day and to meditate day and night on His Word, you will keep your mind stayed on God. Continued meditation on the Word of God produces a great calming effect.

Chapter 13

God Will Bring You Safely through Adversity

Do not allow the seeming complexity of any problem that you face to overwhelm you. Instead, turn to God with absolute certainty that He will bring you safely through that problem. "…the Lord knows how to rescue the godly from trials…" (II Peter 2:9 NIV)

As you grow older, you may be more frustrated by seemingly severe problems than you were when you were younger and you had more vitality and energy and the optimism of youth. You have seen that God lives in your heart. He knows exactly what to do when you face adversity. "God is our Refuge and Strength [mighty and impenetrable to temptation], a very present and well-proved help in trouble." (Psalm 46:1 AMP)

God is your "Refuge and Strength." He is with you at all times. He has proven again and again that He can and will bring you safely through adversity. Trust Him completely.

This verse of Scripture is very important at all times, but this promise is especially important as you grow older. Do not look at adversity through the eyes of a person who is older, tired and possibly not feeling well. Look at every problem from the perspective of God Who lives in your heart. Have absolute certainty that your Father will help you in direct proportion to your faith in

Him. Jesus said, "...it shall be done for you as you have believed." (Matthew 8:13 AMP)

Your faith in God is the key to receiving help from God. God will help you in direct proportion to your faith that He will help you. Believe that God will do what He promises to do. *Do* what He instructs you to do. The Bible speaks of Christians who do not do what the Word of God instructs them to do as "...betraying yourselves [into deception by reasoning contrary to the Truth]." (James 1:22 AMP)

This verse and the amplification explain that you will allow Satan to deceive you to the degree that you think contrary to what the Word of God teaches. Satan is a deceiver (see Revelation 12:9). The Word of God is the Truth (see John 17:17). "Lean on, trust in, and be confident in the Lord with all your heart and mind and do not rely on your own insight or understanding. In all your ways know, recognize, and acknowledge Him, and He will direct and make straight and plain your paths." (Proverbs 3:5-6 AMP)

Place all of your trust and confidence in God. Do *not* rely on the limitations of your human knowledge and understanding. Keep God first at all times. If you do, He will guide you and help you.

You should have absolute faith that God always does what His Word says He will do. "...not one thing has failed of all the good things which the Lord your God promised concerning you. All have come to pass for you; not one thing of them has failed." (Joshua 23:14 AMP)

This verse assures you that *none* of God's promises has ever failed. Every promise from God is completely reliable. You can place all of your trust in God and the supernatural promises He gives you in His Word.

God has given you His Book of Instructions, the Bible, to tell you exactly what He will do whenever you face adversity during the final years of your life and at all other times. You *can* rely totally, completely and absolutely on your loving Father and the promises He has given to you.

You saw in Chapter 8 and again in Chapter 12 that the Word of God is your spiritual food. Do not make the mistake that many people make of not feeding themselves spiritually every day during the final years of their lives. Partake continually of the supernatural spiritual nutrition that your Father has provided for every one of His beloved children who will feast on His Word every day as He instructs you to do (see II Corinthians 4:16 and Ephesians 4:23).

As some people grow older, the problems that they face seem to be much worse than they actually are because they do not have the energy and vitality they used to have. Energize yourself continually with the supernatural Word of God (see Hebrews 4:12 AMP).

If you can even begin to comprehend the magnificence of God's Word, you will be like the psalmist who said, "Your testimonies are wonderful [far exceeding anything conceived by man]; therefore my [penitent] self keeps them [hearing, receiving, loving, and obeying them]." (Psalm 119:129 AMP)

The Word of God is wonderful. The amplification of this verse explains that God's Word is *much* greater than any worldly source of security. Love God's Word. Do what God instructs you to do.

In this chapter you have learned the vital importance of consistently programming yourself with the Word of God. In the next chapter you will learn from God's Word exactly what your Father instructs you to do so that your faith in Him will increase steadily.

Chapter 14

Increase Your Faith in God As You Grow Older

Your loving Father always does exactly what He promises to do. He desires to fulfill every promise in the Bible. God said, "…I am alert and active, watching over My word to perform it." (Jeremiah 1:12 AMP)

God knows exactly what you are going through. He knows whether you have faithfully studied and meditated on His Word. He very much wants to do in your life exactly what His Word says He will do. "…continue to stay with and in the faith [in Christ], well-grounded and settled and steadfast, not shifting or moving away from the hope [which rests on and is inspired by] the glad tidings (the Gospel)…" (Colossians 1:23 AMP)

Is your faith in Jesus Christ deep, strong and unwavering? Is this faith solidly anchored on the Word of God? "…we live by faith, not by sight." (II Corinthians 5:7 NIV)

Do not live "by sight." Every aspect of your life should be solidly anchored on God and His Word, *not* on what does or does not happen in the world. Focus on God and His Word at all times with absolute faith, trust and confidence in Him. "Those who trust in, lean on, and confidently hope in the Lord are like Mount Zion, which cannot be moved but abides and stands fast forever." (Psalm 125:1 AMP)

Mount Zion is a mountain near Jerusalem. The name Zion also is used in the Bible to refer to heaven. Your faith in God should be so deep, strong and unwavering that *nothing* can shake it. Your faith in God should be like Mount Zion which is indestructible.

Do *not* allow any problem that you face to shake your faith in God. If there ever is a time when your faith in God should be strong, this time is during the final years of your life. These years can be quite difficult. The Bible says that you cannot please God if you do not have faith in Him. "…without faith it is impossible to please and be satisfactory to Him. For whoever would come near to God must [necessarily] believe that God exists and that He is the rewarder of those who earnestly and diligently seek Him [out]." (Hebrews 11:6 AMP)

It is *impossible* for you to please God unless you have faith in Him. You cannot have an intimate relationship with God unless you are certain that He is with you and that He will reward you if you strongly desire a close relationship with Him. "Let us all come forward and draw near with true (honest and sincere) hearts in unqualified assurance and absolute conviction engendered by faith (by that leaning of the entire human personality on God in absolute trust and confidence in His power, wisdom, and goodness)" (Hebrews 10:22 AMP)

Please note the word "all" at the beginning of this verse. God wants *every one* of His children to continually draw closer to Him. Have absolute faith in God. We believe that the definition of faith in the amplification of this verse is awesome. Faith is "that leaning of the *entire* human personality on God in *absolute* trust and confidence in His power, wisdom and goodness."

Do you lean every aspect of your life on God? Do you trust God totally, completely and absolutely, regardless of what is happening in your life. Your Father promises to bless you abundantly if you have deep and unwavering faith in Him. "…blessed (happy, fortunate, to be envied) is the man who trusts in You [leaning and believing on You, committing all and confidently looking to You, and that without fear or misgiving]!" (Psalm 84:12 AMP)

Do you trust God so much that you lean on Him and commit everything to Him? Do you trust God so much that you absolutely refuse to give in to fear, regardless of the seeming severity of any problem you face? "He who deals wisely and heeds [God's] word and counsel shall find good, and whoever leans on, trusts in, and is confident in the Lord – happy, blessed, and fortunate is he." (Proverbs 16:20 AMP)

God promises that good things will happen in your life *if* you consistently obey the instructions He has given to you in His Word. He promises to bless you if you trust Him completely. "...he who believes in Him [who adheres to, trusts in, and relies on Him] shall not be put to shame nor be disappointed in his expectations." (Romans 9:33 AMP)

God will never disappoint you if you trust Him completely. God will honor your faith. God often emphasizes through repetition. He says essentially the same thing in the next chapter of Romans. The apostle Paul said, "...No man who believes in Him [who adheres to, relies on, and trusts in Him] will [ever] be put to shame or be disappointed." (Romans 10:11 AMP)

The words "no man" in this verse include *you*. Your Father repeatedly assures you that you will *never* be disappointed if you place all of your trust and confidence in Him. You should be like the psalmist David who said, "The Lord is my Strength and my [impenetrable] Shield; my heart trusts in, relies on, and confidently leans on Him, and I am helped..." (Psalm 28:7 AMP)

God will strengthen you and protect you *if* you trust Him completely. He will help you (see Psalm 121:2, Isaiah 41:13 and Hebrews 4:16 and 13:6). Think positively, not negatively, whenever you face adversity. The theory of positive thinking is correct as far as it goes, but you cannot think positively in the face of severe adversity unless you have a solid foundation for your positive thinking. The Word of God *is* the solid foundation that positive thinking requires to work effectively.

Your Father wants you to stay strong in Him throughout your life, particularly during your final years. If you face difficult problems as you grow older, you will only be able to cope with these problems in proportion to your faith in the God.

Faith in God is not a formula. Faith in God is spontaneous. This faith comes from deep inside of you. Faith is not something that is logically thought out. Faith in God develops as a result of spending a significant amount of time drawing closer to God over a period of weeks, months and years. You saw in Chapter 7 that God's Word in your heart is the foundation for your faith in Him (see Romans 10:8).

Your faith in God connects you with God's supernatural strength. Your Father will strengthen you during the final years of your life if you have a close and intimate relationship with Him. "...be strong in the Lord [be empowered through your union with Him]; draw your strength from Him [that strength which His boundless might provides]." (Ephesians 6:10 AMP)

Receive by faith the supernatural strength that God promises to give you (see Psalm 29:11, Isaiah 40:28-31, II Corinthians 12:9-10 and Philippians 4:13). You will receive His supernatural strength if you are so close to Him that you trust Him completely.

You saw in Chapter 2 that you can turn away from the superficial ways of the world by consistently renewing your mind in God's Word (see Romans 12:2, II Corinthians 4:16 and Ephesians 4:23). Are you on fire for God? Do you consistently immerse yourself in His Word? If you answer these questions affirmatively, you will *not* be defeated by any problem that you face, no matter how old you are or how severe this problem may seem.

Jesus instructs you to trust God just as little children trust their loving parents. He said, "...whoever does not accept and receive and welcome the kingdom of God like a little child [does] shall not in any way enter it [at all]." (Luke 18:17 AMP)

You cannot enter into the kingdom of God unless you enter with simple childlike faith. Faith in God is not complicated and complex. *The older you get, the more childlike you should be.* Most people turn away from the simplicity of childhood as they grow older. Your Father wants you to do just the opposite. If you are growing in the spiritual realm, you should turn more and more back to the simple childlike faith that little children have in their loving parents.

Spiritual maturity and childlike trust go together. The less spiritual maturity you have, the less childlike your trust in God will be. The more spiritually mature you are, the more childlike your faith in God will be.

Little children do not provide for themselves. All of their needs are met by their parents. These children are happy and carefree. They laugh and play. They are not concerned with the problems of life because they trust their parents completely. Have absolute faith in your Father just as little children trust their loving parents.

Do not block God by religious tradition and worldly logic and intellectualism. Jesus said, "…for the sake of your tradition (the rules handed down by your forefathers), you have set aside the Word of God [depriving it of force and authority and making it of no effect]." (Matthew 15:6 AMP)

Turn away from the intellectualism of human understanding. Turn away from traditional worldly thinking. Anchor every aspect of your life on God Who lives in your heart. Fill your heart continually with His supernatural living Word.

The amplification of Matthew 15:6 says that you will make the Word of God "of no effect" if you live your life based on traditional worldly thinking. You must continually transform your thinking by renewing your mind in God's Word each day and by meditating day and night on the Holy Scriptures.

This chapter is filled with several verses of Scripture that explain how to deal with adversity. In the next two chapters you will learn how to live your life one day at a time without being overcome by anything that has happened in the past or by any concerns about what might happen in the future.

Chapter 15

God's Instructions Regarding the Past and the Future

Some older people focus on the past. Today is the first day of the rest of your life. Instead of focusing on what did or did not happen in the past, your Father instructs you to focus on what He is doing in your life now and what He has planned for your future. God says, "Forget the former things; do not dwell on the past. See, I am doing a new thing! Now it springs up; do you not perceive it? I am making a way in the wilderness and streams in the wasteland." (Isaiah 43:18-19 NIV)

Wipe the slate clean. The past is behind you. Visualize God at work molding you, shaping you and changing your life to be what He wants you to be. Trust Him completely to show you the way through whatever adversity you face.

Have you been through difficult times in the past? The following words that were spoken to Job many years ago apply to your life today. "…you shall forget your misery; you shall remember it as waters that pass away. And [your] life shall be clearer than the noonday and rise above it; though there be darkness, it shall be as the morning. And you shall be secure and feel confident because there is hope…" (Job 11:16-18 AMP)

Your Father instructs you to forget any adversity you have suffered in the past. He will give you a fresh new start if you trust Him completely. He does not want you to give up hope. You always will have hope if you focus consistently on Him and place all of your trust and confidence in Him.

George Washington, the first president of the United States, once said, "We ought not to look back unless it is to derive useful lessons from past errors." Learn from your past mistakes. Then move forward with God's plan for the remainder of your life.

Do not feel sorry that you are approaching the final years of your life. Instead, look forward with great anticipation to what your Father has planned from now until you go to be with Him in heaven.

There is one area where the Bible teaches you to focus on regarding the past. God instructs you to focus on the good things He has done in your life and in the lives of others. Believe that God will do good things in your life in the future just as He has done for you and for others in the past. "…stand still and consider the wondrous works of God." (Job 37:14 AMP)

Do not allow yourself to become agitated by any problems you face. Instead, you are instructed to "stand still" as you consider the great things that God has done. "…you shall [earnestly] remember all the way which the Lord your God led you these forty years in the wilderness, to humble you and to prove you, to know what was in your [mind and] heart, whether you would keep His commandments or not." (Deuteronomy 8:2 AMP)

These words that God spoke to the Israelites about bringing them through the wilderness apply to your life today. If you have been a Christian for many years and God has done great things in your life, you can and should focus on these blessings. If you are a relatively new Christian and you have not had successful personal experiences with God, you can focus on the many true stories in the Bible that tell of the great things that God has done.

Believe that God will do great things in your life today and in the future according to your faith in Him. You should be like the psalmist who said, "I will [earnestly] recall the deeds of the Lord; yes, I will [earnestly] remember the wonders [You performed for our fathers] of old. I will meditate also upon all Your works and consider all Your [mighty] deeds." (Psalm 77:11-12 AMP)

You also are instructed to "earnestly remember" the great things that God did for others in the past. When you do something earnestly, you are very intense about what you are doing. Meditate often on what God has done for others. You should be like the psalmist David who said, "On the glorious splendor of Your majesty and on Your wondrous works I will meditate." (Psalm 145:5 AMP)

God is majestic. He does great things. If you are obeying His instructions to renew your mind by studying His Word each day and if you are obeying His instructions to meditate day and night on His Word, you will come across many stories of great things that God has done in the lives of people in the Bible. Believe that God will do great things for *you* during the remainder of your time on earth as well.

We have talked about focusing on times when God has helped you and other people in the Bible. We also recommend that you look carefully at other Christians you know who have received help from God when they were in trouble. If possible, talk with these Christians. Listen to what they say about what God did in their lives. Use their testimony as reinforcement for your faith to believe that God can and will help you now with whatever problems you face.

I (Jack) am 80 years old as I write these words. I have been a Christian for 37 years. I have experienced a great deal of adversity in my life. As I look back, I can truthfully say that virtually all of the problems that I faced actually have turned out to be a blessing (see Romans 8:28).

So far in this chapter we have focused on Scripture pertaining to the past. We now are ready to learn God's instructions pertaining to the future. Are you facing difficult problems as you grow older? Absolutely refuse to be afraid of what might happen in the future. "Fear nothing that you are about to suffer. [Dismiss your dread and your fears!]…" (Revelation 2:10 AMP)

God says that you should not be afraid of anything that might happen to you. Refuse to be worried, anxious and fearful about anything that could happen in the future. Fill your mind and your heart with promises from the supernatural living Word of God. Focus continually on God instead of allowing yourself to dwell on what might happen in the future.

We studied several verses of Scripture in Chapter 11 about God, Jesus Christ and the Holy Spirit living in *your* heart if Jesus Christ is your Savior. Jesus said that the Holy Spirit "…will announce and declare to you the things that are to come [that will happen in the future]." (John 16:13 AMP)

The Holy Spirit knows everything that will happen in the future. Focus on His mighty indwelling presence instead of focusing on anything in the world that mighty cause you to be concerned about the future. Have absolute faith that the Holy Spirit knows exactly what will happen and that He will guide you and bring you safely through whatever the future may hold. Focus continually on Him because you trust Him completely.

If you have faithfully obeyed God's instructions to meditate day and night on His Word, you will have prepared yourself for adversity that you might face in the future. Your mind cannot think of two things at the same time. If you meditate day and night on God's Word, there is no way that you can worry about the future. Jesus said, "…do not worry or be anxious about tomorrow, for tomorrow will have worries and anxieties of its own. Sufficient for each day is its own trouble." (Matthew 6:34 AMP)

Live your life one day at a time, meditating day and night on God and His Word. In the next chapter we will study several verses of Scripture that will explain how your loving Father instructs you to live one day at a time.

Chapter 16

Trust God to Guide You One Day at a Time

We studied Matthew 6:34 at the end of the last chapter. In this verse Jesus told you not to worry about the future. He also said "sufficient for *each day* is its own trouble."

The Bible contains many specific instructions about living one day at a time. Each day is a gift that God has given to you. "This is the day which the LORD hath made; we will rejoice and be glad in it." (Psalm 118:24 KJV)

Your Father instructs you to rejoice in this day that He has given to you. He instructs you to be glad about today. You should look forward to each new day.

I once read about a Canadian physician who instructed his patients to live in "day-tight compartments." When you live in day-tight compartments, you refuse to dwell on the past. You refuse to worry about the future. You focus *entirely* on today.

We see an example of this principle in the following instructions that Jesus gave to His disciples about trusting God to provide their food one day at a time. Jesus said, "Give us each day our daily bread." (Luke 11:3 NIV)

The word "daily" in this verse is important. Jesus did not pray for food for a week or for a month. He prayed for food for one day. Your Father wants you to trust Him to provide for your needs one day at a time. He wants you to live every other aspect of your life one day at a time.

The Bible contains many promises about God giving you strength. God does not promise to strengthen you next week, next month or next year. God promises to strengthen you each day. "…as your day, so shall your strength, your rest and security, be." (Deuteronomy 33:25 AMP)

When you need supernatural strength from God, trust your loving Father to give you the strength that you need to get through today. Rest in Him. Receive the security that He promises to give you with absolute faith that He always does what He says He will do.

The one day at a time principle often can be reduced to living your life one hour at a time. Do not get ahead of God. If you face severe adversity, trust God to bring you safely through the next hour. Do not worry about two hours from now, four hours from now, tonight or tomorrow. Focus on God and meditate on His Word one hour at a time when you face difficult challenges.

Keep your life simple. In addition to living one day at a time and one hour at a time, God often instructs you to take one step at a time. The psalmist David said, "The steps of a [good] man are directed and established by the Lord when He delights in his way [and He busies Himself with his every step]." (Psalm 37:23 AMP)

God wants to direct your steps. He wants to guide you every step of the way as you go through life. Your Father is delighted when you surrender control and allow Him to guide you. "A man's mind plans his way, but the Lord directs his steps and makes them sure." (Proverbs 16:9 AMP)

God does not require you to figure everything out. He instructs you to trust Him to direct your steps. Trust God with every minute detail of your life. He often enables you to see just far enough ahead to take a step to do what is immediately in front of you. He then instructs you to trust Him to direct the next step after that. God said, "My desire is to have you free from all anxiety and distressing care…." (I Corinthians 7:32 AMP)

Your Father wants you to be completely free from *all* worry and anxiety. He wants you to trust Him totally, completely and absolutely. Jesus said, "…be on your guard, lest your hearts be overburdened and depressed (weighed down) with … worldly worries" (Luke 21:34 AMP)

Jesus instructs you to guard against allowing yourself to have a heavy heart that is overloaded with worry about anything that is happening in the world. Turn away from all potential worry and concern. Focus continually on God.

Some people are chronic worriers. They worry about one thing after another, day after day. Jesus spoke to chronic worriers when He said, "…stop being perpetually uneasy (anxious and worried)…" (Matthew 6:25 AMP)

The word "perpetually" in this verse means to do something continually. If you worry a lot, Jesus has one word of instruction for you – STOP. The Word of God contains many instructions telling you not to be worried, anxious or fearful.

If you face challenges with your health as you grow older, close the door to yesterday. Close the door to tomorrow. Live your life one day at a time and, if necessary, one hour at a time. Take the next step that the Lord shows you. Refuse to complicate your life. Jesus said, "Do not let your hearts be troubled (distressed, agitated). You believe in and adhere to and trust in and rely on God; believe in and adhere to and trust in and rely also on Me." (John 14:1 AMP)

Please note the word "let" in this verse. *You decide* what you will allow to enter into your heart. Do not allow yourself to focus on the problems you face today or concerns about the future. Trust God completely. "Do not be anxious about anything, but in every situation, by prayer and petition, with thanksgiving, present your requests to God. And the peace of God, which transcends all understanding, will guard your hearts and your minds in Christ Jesus." (Philippians 4:6-7 NIV)

Once again, God says that you should not be worried or anxious about *anything*. He instructs you to bring *every* problem to Him in prayer. Base your prayers on specific promises from His

Word. *Thank God when you pray* because you have absolute faith that He will do exactly what He promises to do (see Joshua 23:14 and I Corinthians 1:9).

Always go to God with prayers of faith based on specific promises in His Word. If you thank God when you pray because of your absolute faith that He always does what He promises to do, you *will* experience His supernatural peace. This peace is *so* great that it surpasses the limitations of your human understanding.

If you are tempted to be worried or anxious, focus on these verses of Scripture pertaining to worry and anxiety. Pray God's Word back to Him. Trust God completely to do what His Word says He will do. "…put the Lord in remembrance [of His promises], keep not silence" (Isaiah 62:6 AMP)

You are instructed to "put the Lord in remembrance of His promises" when you pray. Thank God in advance for the answer that you are certain He will give you.

If you obey these specific instructions, God's supernatural peace will "guard your heart and your mind." Absolutely refuse to worry about anything. Pray continually. Thank God for answering your prayer. "Blessed be the Lord, Who bears our burdens and carries us day by day…" (Psalm 68:19 AMP)

God promises to bear your burdens. He promises to carry you "day by day." Trust God to carry your burdens one day at a time.

In Chapter 1 we studied Isaiah 46:3-4. You saw that God promises to carry you from your birth through your old age up to the time you go to be with Him in heaven. Simplify your life. Trust God completely instead of thinking that you have to do everything yourself. "…I know that [the determination of] the way of a man is not in himself; it is not in man [even in a strong man or in a man at his best] to direct his [own] steps." (Jeremiah 10:23 AMP)

The amplification of this verse speaks of "a strong man or a man at his best." No matter how much natural ability God has given you, He does not expect you to do everything with your human abilities. Trust Him to direct you each step of the way.

Let go of every problem you face. Trust God completely to solve these problems. "Cast your burden on the Lord [releasing the weight of it] and He will sustain you; He will never allow the [consistently] righteous to be moved (made to slip, fall, or fail)." (Psalm 55:22 AMP)

When you "cast" something, you *throw* it. When you cast a fishing line with a sinker on it, you *throw* that line. You trust the weight of the sinker to carry the line, the hook and the bait out to where you believe fish might be located.

Your Father wants you *throw* your problems to Him. He promises that He will sustain you if you give your problems to Him and trust Him completely to solve these problems. He will *never* allow you to fail if you trust Him totally, completely and absolutely.

Do not be worried and anxious about the problems you face now or about any problems that you might face in the future. "…humble yourselves [demote, lower yourselves in your own estimation] under the mighty hand of God, that in due time He may exalt you, casting the whole of your care [all your anxieties, all your worries, all your concerns, once and for all] on Him, for He cares for you affectionately and cares about you watchfully." (I Peter 5:6-7 AMP)

This verse instructs you to humble yourself before God. You do not have to do everything yourself. Trust God to bring you safely through whatever problems you face in His way and in His good timing. Please note that the word "all" is used four times in the amplification of this passage of Scripture. This amplification instructs you to cast "*all* your anxieties, *all* your worries, *all* your concerns, once and for *all*, on Him."

Your Father cares about you. He loves you. He is watching over you. Do not worry. Trust Him completely. "Commit your way to the Lord [roll and repose each care of your load on Him]; trust (lean on, rely on, and be confident) also in Him and He will bring it to pass." (Psalm 37:5 AMP)

You are instructed to commit your life to God. Give all of your burdens to Him. Trust Him completely. Lean on Him. Have absolute confidence that He will bring you safely through whatever adversity you face.

You decide whether you will trust God to carry the burdens or whether you will struggle trying to make things happen yourself. If you really trust God, you will not struggle and strain. You will do the best you can with your human abilities. Then you will let go and allow God to carry the burdens from there.

God will not *take* your burdens from you. You need to *give* your burdens to Him. You should have so much faith in God that you will *leave* your problems with Him for as long as He requires.

This chapter is filled with important instructions from your Father that tell you how He wants you to live as you grow older. Live one day at a time. Absolutely refuse to be worried and anxious. Give your problems to God. Leave them with Him.

Chapter 17

God Has a Specific Plan for Your Life

In the next three chapters we will look into God's Word for information pertaining to the specific assignment that God has for your life. The psalmist David knew that God had a special plan for every day of his life. David said, "Your eyes saw my unformed substance, and in Your book all the days [of my life] were written before ever they took shape, when as yet there was none of them." (Psalm 139:16 AMP)

Even before God formed David in his mother's womb, He knew exactly what He wanted David to do throughout his life. Is Jesus Christ your Savior? If He is, you can be certain that God has a specific assignment for your life. "...we are God's [own] handiwork (His workmanship), recreated in Christ Jesus, [born anew] that we may do those good works which God predestined (planned beforehand) for us [taking paths which He prepared ahead of time], that we should walk in them [living the good life which He prearranged and made ready for us to live]." (Ephesians 2:10 AMP)

When you received Jesus Christ as your Savior, you were recreated so that you could carry out the assignment that God has for you. If you are growing older, please understand that it is not too late for you to seek, find and carry out God's assignment for the final years of your life. God has a specific plan for your life just as He had a specific plan for David's life.

Look at the years remaining in your life from an eternal perspective. Perhaps you were very busy in the past raising children and fulfilling vocational duties. As you grow older and your children are grown and you have retired from your vocation, you have increased discretionary time that can be devoted toward completing the assignment that God has for you.

When God created you, He gave you specific talents that you did not earn and do not deserve. God gave you these talents to carry out His assignment for your life. "We have different gifts, according to the grace given to each of us. If your gift is prophesying, then prophesy in accordance with your faith; if it is serving, then serve; if it is teaching, then teach; if it is to encourage, then give encouragement; if it is giving, then give generously; if it is to lead, do it diligently; if it is to show mercy, do it cheerfully." (Romans 12:6-8 NIV)

You can see from this passage of Scripture that God has given widely varied talents to all of the people He has created. Your Father wants you to identify and use the specific talents He has given to you to carry out His assignment for the remainder of your life.

God created each person to be unique, special and different. There is no one else in the entire world like you. Every person's fingerprints are unique. In recent years DNA evidence has become important legally because no two people have the same DNA. As you learn more and more about the specific plan that God has for the remainder of your life, you should be determined to use your God-given talents to complete this assignment.

If you do not use the talents and abilities that God has given to you, you waste this precious gift from God. If you are in the final years of your life, we pray that the scriptural instructions in these three chapters will motivate you to fervently seek, find and carry out God's assignment for the remainder of your life.

The Bible does not say much about retirement. The following passage of Scripture will give you an indication of God's general philosophy pertaining to what the world calls retirement. "...the Lord said to Moses, This is what applies to the Levites: from twenty-five years old and upward they shall go in to perform the work of the service of the Tent of Meeting, and at the age of fifty years, they shall retire from the warfare of the service and serve no more, but shall help their brethren in the Tent of Meeting [attend to protecting the sacred things from being profaned], but shall do no regular or heavy service..." (Numbers 8:23-26 AMP)

This passage of Scripture explains that the Levites should work hard at specific duties from the ages of 25 to 50. The Levites were instructed to retire from these duties at the age of 50.

We are not saying that you should retire at the age of 50. However, when you do retire from your vocation, you can be certain that your Father has a specific plan for the remainder of your life. The word "retirement" suggests inactivity. The opposite of the word "retire" is to "aspire." Your Father wants you to *aspire* to do what He has called you to do throughout the remainder of your life.

You probably have learned many valuable lessons during your lifetime. God instructs you to share what you have learned with future generations. "Hear this, you aged men, and give ear, all you inhabitants of the land! Has such a thing as this occurred in your days or even in the days of your fathers? Tell your children of it, and let your children tell their children, and their children another generation." (Joel 1:2-3 AMP)

This passage of Scripture speaks specifically to older people. You are instructed to share what you have learned with your children. They in turn are instructed to share what they learned with future generations. You should be excited about the plan that God has for the remainder of your life. "...if a man should live many years, let him rejoice in them all..." (Ecclesiastes 11:8 AMP)

God instructs you to rejoice if you are living a long life. Thank God and praise Him for the years He has given to you. God created you to live a long, full and productive life. "You shall come to your grave in ripe old age..." (Job 5:26 AMP)

Focus continually on what God has called you to do. Older people should have something to look forward to during the final years of their lives. "...your old men shall dream [divinely suggested] dreams." (Acts 2:17 AMP)

God is speaking specifically to older people in this verse. The amplification explains that your Father will give you "divinely suggested dreams." These dreams often will indicate some aspects of His plan for the remainder of your life. You should have the same attitude that the psalmist had when he said, "…even when I am old and gray-headed, O God, forsake me not, [but keep me alive] until I have declared Your mighty strength to [this] generation, and Your might and power to all that are to come." (Psalm 71:18 AMP)

Do you have a consuming desire to share God with others during the final years of your life? We have this goal as we write these books at our advanced ages. You should have the same attitude that the apostle Paul had when he referred to himself as "…an ambassador [of Christ Jesus] and an old man and now a prisoner for His sake" (Philemon 1:9 AMP)

Paul referred to himself as a prisoner for Jesus Christ. Paul gave up his God-given right to do whatever he chose to do with his life (see I Corinthians 8:9). Paul used the freedom of choice that God gave him wisely. He surrendered control of his life to God. Paul essentially became a prisoner of God who was totally committed to do whatever God wanted him to do with the final years of his life (see Luke 9:23, I Corinthians 11:31, Galatians 2:20 and Ephesians 3:1).

Paul was an old man when he spoke these words. Your Father also wants you to bring forth fruit during the final years of your life. "[Growing in grace] they shall still bring forth fruit in old age; they shall be full of sap [of spiritual vitality] and [rich in the] verdure [of trust, love, and contentment]." (Psalm 92:14 AMP)

Your Father *will* give you grace to produce fruit during the final years of your life. You will experience great contentment if you devote your final years to carrying out God's assignment for your life.

Some older people devote their lives to the pursuit of pleasure. Their lives are relatively idle. They spend a lot of time watching television. They are not devoting their final years to doing what God has called them to do. Be determined that you will *not* waste the final years of your life.

These years can be the best part of your life. The remainder of your life on earth will be meaningful, fulfilling and exciting if you consistently seek, find and carry out God's assignment for your life.

This chapter contains many specific scriptural instructions for older people. In the next two chapters we will look into God's Word for additional instructions pertaining to God's plan for your life.

Chapter 18

Focus Fervently on God's Assignment for Your Life

You have seen that God had a plan for every day of your life before you were born. You have seen the vital importance of fulfilling God's assignment for your life as you grow older. In the next two chapters we will look into God's Word for specific instructions that will tell how to complete God's assignment for your life.

When Jesus explained what we today call the Lord's Prayer, He emphasized that every person earth should seek to do God's will just as every person in heaven does God's will. Jesus said, "...Your will be done [held holy and revered] on earth as it is in heaven." (Luke 11:2 AMP)

The words "held holy and revered" in the amplification of this verse explain the importance that God places on seeking, finding and carrying out His will for your life. Instead of devoting the final years of your life to selfish goals, you should have reverence and awe for God's specific assignment for the remainder of your life.

Jesus is your example in every area of your life. During His earthly ministry Jesus said, "...I do not seek or consult My own will [I have no desire to do what is pleasing to Myself, My own aim, My own purpose] but only the will and pleasure of the Father Who sent Me." (John 5:30 AMP)

The amplification explains that Jesus did not have any desire to do what pleased Him. He did not pursue personal goals. He was totally committed to completing the assignment God had given to Him.

If you sincerely desire to seek, find and carry out God's plan for your life, your Father *will* reveal exactly what He has called you to do. "…the God of our forefathers has destined and appointed you to come progressively to know His will [to perceive, to recognize more strongly and clearly, and to become better and more intimately acquainted with His will]…" (Acts 22:14 AMP)

When something happens progressively, it takes place in successive steps. You will not fully understand every detail of God's will for your life immediately. If you consistently seek God's plan for your life, your Father will progressively reveal more and more of the details pertaining to what He has called you to do.

God knows every minute detail pertaining to the lives of every one of the billions of people on earth (see II Chronicles 28:9, Proverbs 15:3, Psalm 139:1-4 and 147:4 and Hebrews 4:13). He knows how deeply you desire to find and carry out His assignment for your life. Your Father is observing you to see if you will make a firm commitment to carry out His assignment for your life. If you make this commitment, He will progressively reveal the details of what He wants you to do throughout the remainder of your life.

We explained in Chapter 12 that God is omnipresent. He is everywhere at the same time (see Jeremiah 23:24 and Ephesians 4:6). In addition to sitting on His throne in heaven, God lives in the heart of every one of His children. If Jesus Christ is your Savior, God lives in *your* heart. "…it is God Who is all the while effectually at work in you [energizing and creating in you the power and desire], both to will and to work for His good pleasure and satisfaction and delight." (Philippians 2:13 AMP)

This verse explains that God works continually in you. The amplification says that your Father will give you supernatural energy to do what He has called you to do. God will be pleased, satisfied and delighted if you actually seek His will for your life.

You should follow the example of the apostle Paul who said, "...none of these things move me; neither do I esteem my life dear to myself, if only I may finish my course with joy and the ministry which I have obtained from [which was entrusted to me by] the Lord Jesus..." (Acts 20:24 AMP)

Paul knew that he would face severe adversity. He did not allow any adversity he faced to move him. Paul was not focused on personal goals. He focused entirely on joyfully completing the assignment that Jesus gave him.

Do you have a similar deep and fervent desire to devote the remainder of your life to carrying out God's assignment for your life? Is this goal important to you? If you answer these questions affirmatively, you should do what Paul said that the church at Macedonia did when he said, "...first they gave themselves to the Lord and to us [as His agents] by the will of God [entirely disregarding their personal interests, they gave as much as they possibly could, having put themselves at our disposal to be directed by the will of God]" (II Corinthians 8:5 AMP)

These people turned completely away from personal goals. They devoted their lives entirely to carrying out God's will. The psalmist spoke of his dedication to do what God called him to do during the final years of his life. He said, "I shall not die but live, and shall declare the works and recount the illustrious acts of the Lord." (Psalm 118:17 AMP)

The psalmist knew that the time for his death had not yet arrived. He still had work to do for God. He was determined to do what God had called him to do during the final years of his life.

If you have a similar desire, you should obey the advice that Paul gave in his first letter to the Corinthians when he said, "...be firm (steadfast), immovable, always abounding in the work of the Lord [always being superior, excelling, doing more than enough in the service of the Lord], knowing and being continually aware that your labor in the Lord is not futile [it is never wasted or to no purpose]." (I Corinthians 15:58 NIV)

The Word of God instructs you to be strongly focused on doing what God has called you to do. You cannot spend the remainder of your life more profitably. "Never lag in zeal and in earnest endeavor; be aglow and burning with the Spirit, serving the Lord." (Romans 12:11 AMP)

You should have a burning desire to find and successfully complete God's assignment for your life. If you sincerely desire to receive manifestation of God's will for your life, you should go to Him constantly in prayer. You saw in Chapter 16 that God instructs you to "put Him in remembrance of His promises" when you pray. (see Isaiah 62:6 AMP)

Go to God often with the promises from His Word that we are sharing with you here. Pray to God based on specific promises that He has given to you regarding His will for your life. Pray fervently as you consistently ask God to progressively reveal His assignment for the remainder of your life.

Ask God to give you supernatural strength, power and anointing to successfully complete His assignment for your life. "…The earnest (heartfelt, continued) prayer of a righteous man makes tremendous power available [dynamic in its working]." (James 5:16 AMP)

This verse instructs you to pray earnestly. When you do something earnestly, you are very committed to whatever you are doing. The amplification instructs you to pray continually from your heart. If you obey these instructions when you pray, your prayers will release the supernatural power of God to accomplish His plan for your life.

Persevere in your prayers as you repeatedly ask God to show you what He has called you to do with the remainder of your life. Ask God to give you the strength, power and anointing that will be required to accomplish this goal.

You should obey the instructions of Jesus Christ Who said, "…Ask and keep on asking and it shall be given you; seek and keep on seeking and you shall find; knock and keep on knocking and the door shall be opened to you. For everyone who asks and keeps on asking receives; and he who seeks and keeps on seeking finds; and to him who knocks and keeps on knocking, the door shall be opened." (Luke 11:9-10 AMP)

The words "keep on" and "keeps on" are used *six times* in this passage of Scripture. We often say that God emphasizes through repetition. There is no question that you should persevere in your prayers asking God to guide you and anoint you to carry out His assignment for your life.

If you *keep on* asking, you are told that God will respond. If you *keep on* seeking, you will find what you are looking for. If you *keep on* knocking, God will open the door that you are knocking on.

The word "everyone" in Luke 11:10 includes *you*. Persevere in your commitment and your prayers to carry out God's assignment for your life. If you will consistently study and meditate on the Scripture that we are sharing with you, you will be able to progressively understand more about what God has called you to do with the remainder of your life. You will be guided by God to successfully complete this assignment. Your Father wants you to be "…filled with the full (deep and clear) knowledge of His will in all spiritual wisdom [in comprehensive insight into the ways and purposes of God]…" (Colossians 1:9 AMP)

This verse instructs you to be filled with knowledge pertaining to what God has called you to do. Press in to continually learn more about God's plan for your life. The amplification says that God will give you understanding and comprehension about what He wants you to do.

This chapter has been filled with scriptural instruction pertaining to God's will for your life. In the next chapter we will study several additional instructions from God pertaining to His assignment for your life.

Chapter 19

Deep Fulfillment from Being in Partnership with God

How can anything be more important than to do what God has called you to do with your life? *Why* would you ever think that pursuing personal goals can even remotely compare with the eternal significance of doing what God has called you to do? "Look carefully then how you walk! Live purposefully and worthily and accurately, not as the unwise and witless, but as wise (sensible, intelligent people), making the very most of the time [buying up each opportunity], because the days are evil. Therefore do not be vague and thoughtless and foolish, but understanding and firmly grasping what the will of the Lord is." (Ephesians 5:15-17 AMP)

You are instructed to look carefully at how you live. Do not waste the final years of your life. You are instructed to "make the very most" of your life. Do not be "vague and thoughtless and foolish" in regard to God's plan for your life. You are instructed to "understand and fully grasp" what God has called you to do with your life. "…aim at and pursue righteousness (all that is virtuous and good, right living, conformity to the will of God in thought, word, and deed)…" (II Timothy 2:22 AMP)

This verse instructs you to focus on living a righteous life. The amplification instructs you to conform to God's will in your thoughts, words and actions. "Many plans are in a man's mind, but it is the Lord's purpose for him that will stand." (Proverbs 19:21 AMP)

Many peoples' minds are filled with personal goals that have nothing to do with God's plan for their lives. You are told that "it is the Lord's purpose for you that will stand." Focus continually on God's purpose for your life.

We now are ready to look again at a verse of Scripture that we studied in Chapter 2. "Do not be conformed to this world (this age), [fashioned after and adapted to its external, superficial customs], but be transformed (changed) by the [entire] renewal of your mind [by its new ideals and its new attitude], so that you may prove [for yourselves] what is the good and acceptable and perfect will of God, even the thing which is good and acceptable and perfect [in His sight for you]." (Romans 12:2 AMP)

We studied this verse previously in regard to God's instructions to renew your mind consistently to offset the decay that might be taking place in your body as you grow older. You are instructed to turn *away* from the "external, superficial customs" of the world. We now want to look in more detail at the last part of this verse that explains the relationship between continually renewing your mind in God's Word to prove what God has called you to do with your life.

If you are paying the price of filling your mind and your heart with God's Word each day as God has instructed you to do, you will be programming yourself to find God's perfect plan for your life. A computer is ineffective if it is not properly programmed. You must feed the right spiritual data into your mind and your heart to program yourself properly to carry out God's will for your life. You program this vitally important spiritual information from God into your mind and your heart by continually studying and meditating on the instructions that your Father has provided for you.

The following verse of Scripture often is quoted to encourage people when they are going through difficult times. Doing this is correct, but this verse says much more. "We are assured and know that [God being a partner in their labor] all things work together and are [fitting into a plan] for good to and for those who love God and are called according to [His] design and purpose." (Romans 8:28 AMP)

This verse and the amplification say that you can be certain that God is a partner in your labor *if* you are doing what He has called you to do. Some people find that the final years of their lives are not meaningful and fulfilling. They ask themselves, "Is this all there is?" No, there is much more. True fulfillment comes from doing what God created you to do. "...The eye is not satisfied with seeing, nor the ear filled with hearing." (Ecclesiastes 1:8 AMP)

You will never find true meaning and fulfillment in your life through anything in the world that you can discern with your senses. True fulfillment comes from the inside out, not from the outside in. People who consistently pursue worldly goals are doomed to a life of ultimate frustration. "...He also has planted eternity in men's hearts and minds [a divinely implanted sense of a purpose working through the ages which nothing under the sun but God alone can satisfy]..." (Ecclesiastes 3:11 AMP)

This verse explains that God "planted eternity in your heart and your mind" when He created you. God created you in such a way that you will only find true meaning and fulfillment if you are pursuing His assignment for your life. Only God can satisfy any yearning that you have for meaning and fulfillment. "...He satisfies the longing soul and fills the hungry soul with good." (Psalm 107:9 AMP)

True meaning, fulfillment and satisfaction will only come to you if you hunger and thirst for meaning in your life. Your Father will give you glorious meaning, satisfaction and fulfillment during the final years of your life if you will consistently pursue the eternal purpose that He created you for.

God knows what gifts and talents He has given to you. He wants you to devote the remainder of your life to using these gifts and talents to serve Him by carrying out His assignment for your life. Focus your life on the eternal consequences of your life on earth. Look forward to your Father saying to you when you arrive in heaven, "…Well done, good and faithful servant!..." (Matthew 25:21 NIV)

The final years of your life can be very meaningful and fulfilling. John Barrymore was an American actor in the early part of the 20th century. He once said, "A man is not old until regrets take the place of dreams."

Dr. Albert Schweitzer was awarded the Nobel Peace Prize when he was in his late 70s. He was still performing operations in his African hospital at the age of 89. Dr. Schweitzer once said, "I have no intention of dying so long as I can do things for God. If I keep doing things, there is no need to die. So I will live a long, long time!"

I (Jack) am 80 years old as I write this book. I often think of how empty and unfulfilling this stage of my life would be if I was not absolutely certain that I am doing exactly what God created me to do. My value system is focused on God's plan for my life, not on how old I am, how I feel or what other people think of me.

We urge you to fervently pursue God's assignment for your life. Make a firm commitment to make the rest of your life count. You should be like Hudson Taylor who spent more than 50 years as a missionary in China. He once said, "I used to ask God to help me. Then I asked if I might help Him. I ended up asking Him to do His work through me."

We pray that these chapters on God's will for your life will give you encouragement and direction during the final years of your life. You can be certain that God will bless you throughout the remainder of your life and throughout eternity if you are completely focused on serving Him and helping others.

Chapter 20

Be Careful What You Are Hearing

Each of the first nineteen chapters of this book has been solidly anchored on Scripture. Every principle that we have explained has been anchored on the Word of God.

The next six chapters will contain many of our personal opinions that will not be backed up by Scripture. We will include some Scripture in these chapters. However, many of the concepts we will share with you will be our advice on growing older that we have learned from personal experience.

The next six chapters primarily will cover what we have learned about good health. In this chapter we will explain why we believe that some older people have problems that are caused by of indiscriminate television watching.

Most retired people find that they have much more discretionary time each week than they had during their working years. Many of these senior citizens spend a significant amount of this time watching television. A recent survey by *US News and World Report* showed that people aged 65 to 74 watch television approximately 24 hours each week. Seniors aged 75 and older watch television more than 28 hours each week.

In Chapter 2 we explained several verses of Scripture about consistently renewing your mind by studying God's Word each day. In Chapter 5 we explained several verses of Scripture pertaining to meditating day and night on God's Word.

You *will* develop a high level of spiritual maturity if you consistently renew your mind by studying God's Word each day and if you consistently meditate day and night on God's Word. This spiritual maturity will include significantly increased spiritual sensitivity that will enable you to comprehend the principles we will explain in this chapter.

We will begin with the one verse of Scripture that will be the theme verse for this chapter. Jesus Christ said, "…Be careful what you are hearing..." (Mark 4:24 AMP)

These words that Jesus spoke referred primarily to the Word of God. Ideally, your ears should hear your mouth consistently speaking the Word of God as you obey your Father's instructions to meditate day and night on His Word. You learned in Chapter 9 that your faith will increase when your ears consistently *hear* the Word of God (see Romans 10:17). On the other hand, if your ears consistently hear words that are in opposition to the Word of God, your faith in God will be weakened.

You should be very careful about what you allow to come into your ears and also what you allow to enter into your eyes (see Proverbs 4:20-21). Many people spend large amounts of time watching television programs that contain a great deal of violence. They watch many news programs that contain a continual outpouring of bad news about rapes, robberies, murders, and other negative events.

The topics of many television programs lead viewers to accept ungodly behavior and speech. Your television watching should be tested by the Word of God. You must not allow the words or the pictures to contaminate your mind.

Some elderly people watch television so much that their thinking is significantly influenced by television. Some senior citizens who watch television indiscriminately have no sensitivity as to how much their eyes and their ears are constantly being bombarded with words that not only do not line up with the Word of God, but are in direct opposition to the Word of God.

We are *not* suggesting that you stop watching television entirely. Both of us watch television. I (Jack) watch sports, weather and selected Christian television programs. I also spend a great deal of my recreational time enjoying our collection of Christian worship music videos.

Almost 100 of the videos are from Gaither Music. We highly recommend these videos from Bill and Gloria Gaither. If you are interested in learning more, go to www.gaither.com or call 1-800-955-8746 and ask for their latest catalog.

Judy sometimes watches these videos with me. She watches many educational programs that are beneficial to her. Judy has parental block on her television so most of the channels are not received.

Robert Kubey, a psychologist at Rutgers University, performed a study that explained the dependence that many people have on television. Dr. Kubey stated that many people use television as a sedative. Their addiction to watching television fits the criteria for substance abuse that was specifically defined in a psychiatric manual authored by Dr. Kubey.

We first heard national criticism of television in 1961. Newton Minow, who was appointed chairman of the Federal Communication Commission by President John F. Kennedy, referred to television in a speech to the FCC as a "vast wasteland." If Mr. Minow thought that television was a "vast wasteland" back in 1961, what would he conclude about television today with hundreds of channels that televise 24 hours a day?

A survey by the American Journal of Public Health indicated that one-third of American adults are overweight. Many people eat a lot of junk food when they watch television. This study stated that an adult who watches more than three hours of television a day is far more likely to be obese than an adult who watches less than one hour of television per day.

TV Free America said that the average person by the age of 65 has seen more than *two million television commercials*. Most senior citizens have no concept of the cumulative influence that this constant barrage of television commercials has had on their lives.

Those of us who have watched television since its inception have seen a tremendous increase in the number of commercials. In the 1960s a typical 1-hour program would run for 51 minutes with 9 minutes of commercials. Today a 1-hour program runs for 42 minutes with 18 minutes of commercials.

American television viewers now are seeing twice as many commercials as television viewers saw in the 1960s. In the 1960s the average length of a commercial was one minute. As the years have gone by, the average length of an advertisement has been reduced to less than 30 seconds, but *more* of these advertisements are shown during a television break. Television watchers consistently are hammered by one commercial after another after another.

When I watch sports on television, I always mute commercials. I do not want my ears to be hammered by a constant barrage of commercials. I do not want to constantly be told to buy this, to buy that, to do this, to do that or to go here and to go there. Sometimes I watch these commercials even though I don't listen to them. Sometimes just watching them is so detrimental that I turn my eyes away until the commercial is over.

If you have paid the price of obeying God's instructions to consistently renew your mind in His Word and to meditate day and night on the holy Scriptures, you will find that much of what is on television today is very distasteful to you. If you have programmed your mind to think the way that God thinks (see Isaiah 55:8-9), you often will wonder how some people can indiscriminately watch and listen to the barrage of worldly programming and commercials that pours out of their television sets 24 hours a day.

I refuse to watch news on television. I do not want my eyes and my ears to constantly be bombarded with an outpouring of the massive amount of bad news of the world. I do not want to be ignorant of what is going on in the world. I scan the headlines of my daily newspaper to keep myself informed as to what is happening. I then read articles that interest me because of the headline. I also read the daily devotional that Bill Keller writes (see LivePrayer.com).

Many senior citizens do not understand the degree of their addiction to television. Television is a compulsive habit that dominates their lives. Many people watch a lot of television because they do not know what else to do with their time. Some people watch television because they are lonely.

This book contains many specific scriptural instructions that tell you exactly how your Father instructs you to spend your time during your final years. You cannot renew your mind in the Word of God each day and obey God's instructions to consistently turn away from the world and watch television indiscriminately for several hours each day.

Chapter 21

God's Instructions for Health and Healing

Once again we want to say that the next five chapters are based primarily on our opinion. We want to emphasize that there is a vast difference between any obligation you might have to do what God instructed you to do in the first nineteen chapters of this book and to do what we recommend in these chapters.

We are giving you suggestions based on our experience as senior citizens and the things that we have learned about health and healing. We pray that our comments in these chapters will be helpful to you as you grow older.

We will begin this chapter by looking at three passages of Scripture pertaining to your health. First, we will look again at a verse that we previously studied in Chapter 12. "A calm and undisturbed mind and heart are the life and health of the body..." (Proverbs 14:30 AMP)

There is a direct relationship between your physical health and the relative calmness in your mind and your heart when you face adversity. Stress-related illness has increased significantly in recent years. You ultimately will pay a significant price in your health if you do not learn and obey God's specific instructions for dealing with stress. Your health will be much better during the final years of your life *if* your faith in God is deep, strong and unwavering and *if* you learn from the Word of God how to remain calm, quiet and confident in the face of adversity.

We have repeatedly explained the vital importance of renewing your mind in God's Word each day and meditating day and night on the holy Scriptures. If you consistently fill your eyes, your ears, your mind, your heart and your mouth with the supernatural living Word of God, the quality of the final years of your life and the health of your body will be greatly improved. There is a direct relationship between your physical health, the length and quality of your life and the calmness and quietness that exists in your mind and your heart because you have paid the price to learn and obey specific instructions from God.

The following instructions from God explain the relationship between fearing God and your health. "Do not be wise in your own eyes; fear the LORD and shun evil. This will bring health to your body and nourishment to your bones." (Proverbs 3:7-8 NIV)

You are instructed to turn away from the limitations of human wisdom. If you truly fear God, your obedience to His instructions about fearing Him will have a significant effect on the health of your body. When you fear God, you hold Him in reverent awe at all times. Every aspect of your life revolves around your continual consciousness of His indwelling presence. Your mind and your heart are filled with His Word. If you truly fear God, you will turn away from evil. You will not give in to the temptations of Satan and his demons.

There is no question that there is a definite relationship between fearing God and the health of your body. Your health will be much better if you keep God in first place in your life at all times (see Matthew 6:33, John 3:30 and Colossians 1:18) and every other area of your life revolves around your awe and reverence for Him.

The following words that King Solomon spoke to his son also are God's words to you today. "My son, attend to my words; consent and submit to my sayings. Let them not depart from your sight; keep them in the center of your heart. For they are life to those who find them, healing and health to all their flesh. Keep and guard your heart with all vigilance and above all that you guard, for out of it flow the springs of life." (Proverbs 4:20-23 AMP)

The words "attend to my words" mean that you should pay close attention to the Word of God. You are instructed to consistently keep God's Word in front of your eyes. We believe that these words refer to God's instructions to meditate day and night on His Word. If you consistently meditate on God's Word, your heart will be filled with the Word of God. You will obey God's instructions.

If you consistently obey God's instructions, you will experience "healing and health." This promise is especially important during the final years of your life. Your heart is the key to your life (see Proverbs 23:7). You are instructed to carefully guard what you allow to enter into your heart. You are instructed to do this *"above all* that you guard." There is no question that there is a definite relationship between a heart that is filled with the Word of God and your physical health.

We now would like to briefly examine what the Bible says about the supernatural healing that God has provided for you if you are sick. "Surely He has borne our griefs (sicknesses, weaknesses, and distresses) and carried our sorrows and pains [of punishment], yet we [ignorantly] considered Him stricken, smitten, and afflicted by God [as if with leprosy]. But He was wounded for our transgressions, He was bruised for our guilt and iniquities; the chastisement [needful to obtain] peace and well-being for us was upon Him, and with the stripes [that wounded] Him we are healed and made whole." (Isaiah 53:4-5 AMP)

These prophetic words from Isaiah refer to Jesus Christ. Jesus "surely has borne your griefs (*including* sickness)." Jesus was wounded for *you*. He was taken to a whipping post where Roman soldiers whipped Him mercilessly. The stripes that their whiplashes put on His body enable *you* to be "healed and made whole."

These prophetic words that Isaiah spoke in the Old Testament are confirmed in the following Scripture reference from the New Testament. "Who his own self bare our sins in his own body on the tree, that we, being dead to sins, should live unto righteousness: by whose stripes ye were healed." (I Peter 2:24 KJV)

This verse applies to the enormous price that Jesus paid for forgiveness of your sins and healing your body. Jesus not only bore the price of your sins on the tree, which refers to being crucified on the cross, but He also provided healing for your body when He was brutally whipped by Roman soldiers. By His stripes "you *were* healed." The word "were" in this verse indicates that you already have been healed of sickness. Jesus has paid the full price for all of your sins *and* for healing of sickness in your body (see Isaiah 52:14).

If you do not feel well as you grow older, you should not spend a significant amount of time talking about your symptoms. You may have to speak occasionally about the symptoms of sickness in your body to answer questions from a physician or another health specialist. You may have to speak occasionally about the symptoms of sickness to members of your family so that they will know exactly where you stand. With these exceptions, you should consistently speak healing promises from the Word of God. The words that come out of your mouth in regard to your health should line up with God's Word. "…the tongue of the wise brings healing." (Proverbs 12:18 AMP)

There is no question that there is a definite relationship between the words that you habitually speak and receiving healing from God. "Pleasant words are as a honeycomb, sweet to the mind and healing to the body." (Proverbs 16:24 AMP)

You can see from this verse that there is a relationship between the words that you speak and receiving healing in your body. You must understand that the Great Physician lives inside of you (see Zephaniah 3:17, I Corinthians 3:16, II Corinthians 13:5, Ephesians 3:17 and Colossians 2:10). If Jesus Christ is your Savior, the greatest physician Who has ever lived lives in your heart. He is with you throughout every minute of every hour of every day of your life.

We now want to look again at a passage of Scripture that we studied in Chapter 7. This time we will emphasize how this scriptural instruction applies to receiving healing in your body. Jesus said, "…out of the fullness (the overflow, the superabundance) of the heart the mouth speaks. The good man from his inner good treasure flings forth good things, and the evil man out of his inner evil storehouse flings forth evil things." (Matthew 12:34-35 AMP)

The words that consistently come out of your mouth when you are sick or when you face any other adversity will be determined by what you truly believe in your heart. If your heart is filled with God's Word, the Word of God will consistently flow out of your mouth. Instead of continually talking about the pain and discomfort in your body, you will speak words that ultimately will have a significant effect on healing in your body and on your overall health.

We have written a book pertaining to divine healing that is filled with more than 500 verses of Scripture. This book, *Receive Healing from the Lord*, contains many specific instructions and promises from God regarding healing. Please see the comments on *Receive Healing from the Lord* at the beginning of this book. Our website, lamplight.net, contains many additional testimonies pertaining to this book.

If you are a senior citizen and you need physical healing, you might want to purchase a copy of *Receive Healing from the Lord* to consistently study and meditate on the Scripture that is contained in this book. If you are interested in doing this, please see the order form at the back of this book or you can order online.

We also have co-authored a set of Scripture Meditation Cards that also is titled *Receive Healing from the Lord*. Please see the comments on these Scripture cards at the beginning of this book and on our website.

You have learned that God instructs you to meditate day and night on His Word. This set of 52 Scripture cards contains almost 80 verses of Scripture pertaining to physical healing. You can easily carry these cards with you wherever you go so that you can meditate day and night on God's Word pertaining to healing.

In the following chapters I will share what I have learned as a senior citizen in regard to physical health. However, my qualifications to teach on health are not even close to what Judy has to offer.

Judy is 73 years old. She does not look anywhere near this age. A bank employee recently asked Judy for proof that she was older than age 59-1/2 years. A few years ago, the pastor in our church asked how many people in the audience had more energy at that time than they had 20 years ago. Two people raised their hands. Judy was one of them.

Judy is blessed with a great deal of energy because of what she has learned about physical health over the years. Judy began studying health and fitness at age 21. She has continued to study these areas for more than 50 years. The many bookcases in our home are filled with Bible study books and books on health and fitness. Judy is a perpetual learner.

Two weeks before her 73rd birthday, Judy entered a 5K race while visiting our family in North Carolina. She finished in first place for entrants in her age bracket. Several of our grandchildren and other family members cheered for Judy during the race and as she crossed the finish line.

Judy passed the examination to be a Certified Personal Trainer at age 69. She has taught many classes on health and fitness. Judy is in excellent health. She also does not take any medications. We believe that her input to this book is vitally important.

Chapter 22

A Simple and Effective Way to Exercise

In the next two chapters we will share several concepts with you regarding a simple, inexpensive and effective exercise program and how this exercise program can relate to a longer and a healthier life. We now are ready to look again at a verse of Scripture that we studied in Chapter 9. "… physical training is of some value (useful for a little), but godliness (spiritual training) is useful and of value in everything and in every way, for it holds promise for the present life and also for the life which is to come." (I Timothy 4:8 AMP)

We previously studied this verse to explain how much more important spiritual exercise is than physical exercise. The emphasis on spiritual exercise over physical exercise is because exercising your spirit has eternal significance while physical training applies to the remainder of your life on earth. We believe that the information we will share in the next two chapters will help many people to develop an exercise program that will help them throughout the remainder of their lives on earth.

These two chapters will deal primarily with walking. The reason that I (Jack) have written primarily on this subject is because walking is the physical exercise I have been doing for the past 40 years. I have been blessed abundantly by walking. Even if you are not interested in walking as your chosen way to exercise, I hope you will read these chapters with an open mind. We believe that several of the principles that we will explain will apply to any effective exercise program.

First, I would like to give you a brief history of how I have walked over the years and the tremendous benefits I have obtained. Walking was a big part of my life when I was a boy in Vermont in the 1940s. There were no school buses then. I didn't ride my bicycle to school because the school did not have a place to keep bicycles. Also, the weather during the school year often was too cold and snowy to ride a bicycle. I walked every day to school, 30 minutes each way.

I started caddying at a golf course when I was 13 years old. I rode my bicycle approximately 5 times a week for 30 minutes each way to the golf course. I then carried 2 bags of golf clubs for 18 holes (approximately 5 miles of walking). On Saturdays I sometimes would caddy a second 18 holes in the afternoon. Then I would ride my bicycle back home for another 30 minutes. On these days I walked approximately 10 miles and rode my bicycle for approximately an hour.

I was in excellent physical condition as a boy because of all of this exercise. I continued to be in good physical condition when I attended college and during the time I was in the army. However, from shortly after the time I left the army until our children were teenagers, my energy was devoted almost entirely to marriage, children and business. I stopped the walking that had been so beneficial to me for many years.

At the age of 41 I realized that I soon would be in big trouble if I did not start an exercise program and stick to my goals. I started walking again 40 years ago. I have walked consistently ever since that time.

Today as I approach my 81st birthday, I do not walk as fast or as far as I previously did. However, I average walking approximately 30 minutes a day, 6 or 7 days a week. I enjoy taking our dog J.C. with me on these walks.

J.C. gets very excited when he knows we are about to go for a walk. His tail wags repeatedly. He jumps and leaps as we approach the door to go out on our walk. (J.C. is a happy dog. He wags his tail constantly. Sometimes he even wags his tail in his sleep.)

My walking time also is spiritually significant. I pray consistently when I walk. I also praise the Lord and worship Him as I exercise.

In this chapter we will share with you several quotations from well-known people that explain how walking benefited them. Thomas Jefferson, the third president of the United States, said, "The sovereign invigorator of the body is exercise, and of all exercises, walking is the best." Charles Dickens, a nineteenth century English novelist, once said, "The best way to lengthen out our days is to walk steadily and with a purpose."

I am certain that I would not be alive today if I had not walked so consistently during the last 40 years. Our son, David, has seen me walk for many years. When he sent a birthday card on my 80th birthday Dave said, "Congratulations on walking yourself to age 80."

I know that there definitely is a relationship between an effective exercise program and a long and healthy life. I am not saying that walking is the only way to exercise. I am merely sharing with you the exercise I have done in my life.

We all know that bad habits are hard to break. I have found that good habits are just as difficult to break. I keep careful records on my walking. The habit of walking six or seven days each week is so deeply ingrained that I would not even consider not walking consistently. Walking has been *very* beneficial to me.

Jesus Christ is our example in every area of life. Jesus was not a pale, weak man during His earthly ministry. Some artists have portrayed Him in this way, but I believe that these pictures are inaccurate.

Jesus was the son of a carpenter. Although the Bible does not tell us specifically, most Bible students believe that Jesus probably worked as a carpenter during His late teens and throughout His adult years until He began His earthly ministry at the age of 30. Many children at that time worked at the same occupation as their father. I believe it is reasonable to assume that Jesus worked as a carpenter.

In those days carpenters went out into the forest, cut down trees and carried them back. Anyone who was a carpenter was in excellent physical condition. Jesus probably hauled lumber for approximately 15 years from the age of 15 until the age of 30. I believe that Jesus was a strong and robust man with a great deal of energy and vitality.

Jesus and His disciples did a lot of walking in the hills surrounding Jerusalem. The 15th chapter of Matthew explains one instance where Jesus apparently did a lot of walking. Matthew 15:21 says that Jesus withdrew from Gennesaret to Tyre and Sidon. A map of this area will show that these locations are approximately 50 miles apart. Jesus very likely traveled on this 50-mile journey the same way that He went everywhere else – by foot.

If you would be interested in how far Jesus walked during His earthly ministry, look at a map in a study Bible. You can see His journeys traced out on these maps. We believe you will be surprised when you see how far Jesus walked.

The apostle Paul also did a lot of walking On one occasion Paul sent his companions ahead by ship. He then walked a long distance to meet them. "…going on ahead to the ship, the rest of us set sail for Assos, intending to take Paul aboard there, for that was what he had directed, intending himself to go by land [on foot]." (Acts 20:13 AMP)

There is no question that Jesus, Paul and other Christians walked many miles. We see an example of a modern-day Christian leader who benefited greatly from walking in the life of Dr. Billy Graham.

Dr. Graham often became tired in the afternoon when he was in his mid-forties. He knew that this fatigue must be overcome because of his heavy schedule of crusades. He decided to begin a program of walking that soon resulted in overcoming afternoon fatigue.

Abraham Lincoln was one of the greatest presidents of the United States. Before he was elected president, Abraham Lincoln spent many hours walking around the outskirts of his home town of Springfield, Illinois. Mr. Lincoln once said that some of his best thinking took place when he was walking.

When Harry Truman was president of the United States, he usually arose at 5:30 a.m. to go for a brisk walk. Several members of the Washington press corps accompanied him. Sometimes the members of the press tried to interview President Truman while he walked. Many of these reporters could not keep up with his fast pace even though most of them were much younger than he was.

When President Truman was asked why he walked briskly each day he said, "I believe that it will make me live longer." Mr. Truman lived until the age of 87.

Ralph Waldo Emerson, a 19th century American essayist, poet and lecturer, once wrote an essay titled, "Notes on Walking." In this essay Mr. Emerson said, "A walk in the woods is one of the secrets to dodging old age." Mr. Emerson walked almost every day. He was very active until his death at the age of 80.

Many leaders are walkers. Hippocrates, an ancient Greek physician who often has been referred to as the father of medicine, once said, "Walking is man's best medicine." Historians indicate that Socrates, Plato and Aristotle all were walkers.

I am not speaking against health clubs. However, I have found that I can get all the exercise I need just by taking an enjoyable walk six or seven days a week.

Walking is simple, effective and inexpensive. If you decide to start a walking program, you probably can walk close to where you live. You will not need to drive anywhere in your car. You will not need to pay health club dues. You can take a stopwatch with you to monitor your progress to achieve whatever walking goal you have.

At one time I walked 60 minutes a day. Then I cut my walking time down to 45 minutes a day. Now that I am approaching the age of 81, I find that approximately 30 minutes a day is just about right for me.

I carry a stopwatch to keep track of the time that I walk. In the past I walked in many different areas away from our home. I often walked to nearby housing developments. I now walk almost exclusively in the housing development where Judy and I live.

I am excited about walking. I do not have any specific time for my daily walk. I prefer to walk early in the morning whenever I can. Sometimes I walk in the afternoon. I occasionally walk early in the evening.

I would advise you to experiment to find the best time for you to walk. I am now retired from business, although I am very active with Lamplight Ministries. When I was a businessman, I often went for walks when I faced a stressful situation.

I can remember many occasions when I was in business in New Hampshire and I was tense because of business problems. I told my secretary that I was going out. I then would walk for at least 30 minutes in the area immediately surrounding our office. When I came back, I inevitably was more relaxed. I was able to cope much more effectively with whatever stressful situation I faced.

Walking does not require special equipment. I have worn New Balance walking shoes for many years. However, besides the shoes, I wear the same clothing that I wear around the house. I love to get out and walk. Walking is therapeutic. It is energizing. It is relaxing.

If you are interested in starting a walking program, you should start slowly. Take a short walk the first day. Do not walk fast at first. Then, as the days go by, you can increase both the distance and the speed until you find what works best for you.

When I lived in New Hampshire, I often walked inside during stormy weather. I do the same on rainy days here in Florida. Our house in Florida is a one-story home. I can walk effectively in our home just as I did in New Hampshire. Sometimes I listen to worship music to offset the boredom of walking back and forth in the same place. I use my stopwatch to be certain that I make my exercise goals regardless of the weather.

I have never used a treadmill, so I cannot comment on this method of exercising. Through trial and error I believe you will find the best place for you to walk both inside and outside. Sometimes I go to a nearby shopping mall to walk. Many people walk in malls.

I would like to comment briefly on jogging versus walking. Jogging is an excellent form of exercise for many younger people who are not overweight. I was 41 years old and overweight when I started walking 40 years ago. I knew that my body could not tolerate the impact of jogging. I soon learned that I could walk briskly and get almost as much aerobic exercise as I could if I jogged.

This chapter is filled with information pertaining to walking. In the next chapter we will discuss several additional aspects of an effective exercise program. Once again, I am certain that I would not be alive today if I had not walked vigorously and consistently during the past 40 years.

Chapter 23

The Physical and Psychological Benefits of Exercise

In the last chapter we focused almost entirely on walking. In this chapter we will talk about exercise in more general terms. No matter what type of exercise program you choose, you should have definite and specific goals. The apostle Paul said, "... I do not run uncertainly (without definite aim)...." (I Corinthians 9:26 AMP)

There is no question that Paul was referring to keeping his body controlled by his spirit as you can see in the next verse. Paul said, "... [like a boxer] I buffet my body [handle it roughly, discipline it by hardships] and subdue it, for fear that after proclaiming to others the Gospel and things pertaining to it, I myself should become unfit [not stand the test, be unapproved and rejected as a counterfeit]." (I Corinthians 9:27 AMP)

Paul buffeted his body. The amplification explains that Paul did this by punishing his body. Paul emphasized that his goal was to subdue his body. He did this because he did not want to preach the Gospel to others without being physically fit himself. Paul understood the importance of being in good spiritual condition and good physical condition.

Studies have shown that more than half of the people who begin an exercise program quit within a short period of time. They begin with good intentions, but they do not stick to their initial commitment.

I believe there is a much lower drop-out rate among walkers than there is with people who engage in other more vigorous forms of exercise. If you will give walking a fair chance for a month or two, I believe you will be convinced that walking truly is the exercise of a lifetime.

Walking is fun. Give your daily walk the priority that it deserves. Stick with your walking until you learn how enjoyable it can be. If you do, you will not stop.

As you grow older, you do not have the margin for error that you had when you were younger. Younger people often can get by for many years without exercising. As you grow older, you should find a definite and specific exercise program that you enjoy and look forward to doing regularly.

I now would like to mention an alternative form of exercise that both Judy and I use. That is the rebounder. A rebounder is a mini-trampoline. We both use a rebounder on a semi-regular basis.

The springs in a rebounder are what make rebounding such an effective method of exercise. Studies have shown that a rebounder is three to five times as beneficial as the same exercise on the ground. The reason is that the springs provide substantial additional exercise benefits.

When you rebound, the springs absorb your weight and push your body back into the air. Rebounding will give you excellent exercise without any jarring effect. I am able to do exercises on a rebounder that I could not do on the ground.

Sometimes I jog slowly on my rebounder. Sometimes I jump up and down. Judy jogs slowly on her rebounder. Then she jogs as fast as she can for awhile. Then she jogs slowly again. She does interval training. She also exercises with a jump rope on her rebounder. She jumps in the air and clicks her heels together.

We are convinced that rebounding is a great way to exercise. Rebounding was created by NASA for astronauts. When you rebound, you are exercising every cell in your body.

God created your body to move. The lymph system in your body requires movement to function optimally because it has no pump. Its job is to bathe, bring nutrients and remove waste from each cell. Without movement, the cells are starved for nutrients and filled with waste. The result can be cancer, arthritis and other degenerative diseases, plus more rapid aging. Rebounding can increase the lymph flow in your body substantially.

We believe that Needak rebounders are the best (see needak.com). This company is great. Their rebounders have a lot more give than some cheaper rebounders that may jar your back. There is a rebounder for people who are extremely overweight. If you are unsteady at all, you can purchase a metal bar that goes across the rebounder to steady yourself while you exercise. Needak produces many DVDs that you can use while you rebound.

We have two Needak rebounders in our home. Judy has one in her office which is in a guest bedroom at one end of the home. My office is in a bedroom at the other end of the home. The rebounder that I use is in the living room next to my office.

I often use a rebounder on rainy days. Sometimes I use it when I feel a little sluggish and I need a quick burst of energy. I have found that one of the best ways to receive energy is to spend energy. A brief amount of time on a rebounder often revitalizes me.

If you decide to purchase a rebounder, I strongly recommend that you begin *very* gradually. The first time that I used a rebounder, I jogged on it for almost 30 minutes. This was a major mistake. I suffered from severe aches and pains for several days.

We now would like to share with you what we have learned over the years about the value of perspiring as the result of exercise. When the Bible was written, many people perspired heavily each day as a result of their daily work. They went out in the fields and perspired as they worked to earn the food they ate.

Today, very few people perspire as a result of their vocation. God intended for you to work hard enough to perspire. He said, "In the sweat of your face shall you eat bread…" (Genesis 3:19 AMP)

This verse explains the relationship between perspiring while working in the fields and being able to eat food. When God created you, He gave you skin that is filled with thousands of sweat glands. Each of these sweat glands is like a small kidney. When you perspire as a result of exercise, this elimination of waste takes a load off your kidneys and your bowels.

The skin is the largest eliminative organ in your body. If you exercise enough to perspire freely, your skin can eliminate a great deal of waste material. Perspiration often smells bad because you are flushing toxins out of your body when you perspire.

Chemical analysis of perspiration shows that perspiration contains many of the same ingredients as urine. Vigorous exercise will help you to get poisonous waste out of your body through perspiration. Your cells are able to remove toxins from your body when you perspire freely as a result of exercising.

I often walk in warm and humid weather here in Florida. I perspire heavily in the spring and summer months. In the colder weather, I often dress warmly so that I will perspire.

Perspiration enables you to get rid of accumulated salt that builds up in your body. You undoubtedly have seen clothing that was stained by salt from perspiration. Some people consume more salt than their kidneys can remove. When you perspire, you help your kidneys by getting rid of this excess salt.

Bowel movements, urination and perspiration often have a strong odor. This odor gives you an indication of the poison that comes out of a body that is filled with toxins. "…let us cleanse ourselves from everything that contaminates and defiles body and spirit…" (II Corinthians 7:1 AMP)

Please note that this verse instructs you to "cleanse yourself from *everything* that contaminates and defiles *body* and spirit." The Bible study and Scripture meditation that we explained earlier in this book tell you how to cleanse yourself spiritually. Consistent physical exercise will help to cleanse your body.

Some advertisements for deodorants infer that perspiration is bad. Just the opposite is true. Perspiration as a result of exercise is good for you.

We believe you should be careful about using deodorants that contain chemicals. Some of these deodorants plug up your pores and hold poison in that your body desires to remove through perspiration. Using deodorants that contain these chemicals does not make good sense.

I love to perspire. I have learned through many years of walking that I always feel good after I have finished walking and I am perspiring freely. Heavy perspiration will encourage you to drink water.

There is no question that drinking water is beneficial to your body. When you perspire and replace this perspiration by drinking pure water, you are flushing poisonous toxins out of your body and replacing what was flushed out with water. We recommend drinking distilled water or purified water so that you can do the best possible job of cleansing and detoxifying your body.

I am very conscious of how much water I drink each day. Several years ago a Christian physician emphasized to me the importance of drinking a lot of water. He showed me a pitcher of water that he kept on his desk. He said that he drank from this pitcher several times each day.

Ever since that time I have kept records of the amount of water that I estimate I drink each day. I write down how much water I drink in the morning, in the afternoon and in the evening. I try to drink at least two quarts of purified water each day. Sometimes I drink more.

I would like to close this chapter with several paragraphs pertaining to the *tranquilizing effect* that can be obtained from walking. I am not saying that only walking produces these tranquilizing effects. However, you soon will see that several well-known people have commented on the relationship between walking and creativity.

The rhythmic gait of a brisk walk is very relaxing. If you are angry or upset, try going for a brisk walk. You will find that you often cannot maintain a negative attitude while you are walking briskly. I have often gone for a walk when I faced difficult challenges. Even though the problems did not change, my reaction to these problems changed significantly before the walk was completed.

I have found that I receive physical, mental, emotional and psychological benefits from walking. A brisk walk can drain away the effects of stress in a short period of time. Walking is a safety valve. Try walking. See for yourself. After you walk briskly for five or ten minutes, we believe you will find that some of the tension begins to drain away.

In recent years many psychiatrists and clinical psychologists have advised their patients to walk to relieve mental and emotional stress. Dr. Paul Dudley White became famous when he was the physician to President Dwight Eisenhower.

Dr. White once said, "A five-mile walk will do more good to an unhappy but healthy adult than all the medicine and psychology in the world. Vigorous exercise is the best antidote for any nervous or emotional stress that we possess, far better than tranquilizers and sedatives to which unhappily so many people are addicted today."

Dr. Oliver Wendell Holmes, a 19th century American author, physician and lecturer, made an interesting statement about walking. Dr. Holmes said, "In walking, the muscles are so accustomed to working together and perform their task with so little expenditure of force that the intellect is left comparatively free."

Ralph Waldo Emerson attributed some of his creativity to walking. He said, "Walking has the best value as gymnastics of the mind." Henry David Thoreau said, "The moment my legs begin to move, my thoughts begin to flow."

There is no question that walking increases creativity for many people. Both Thomas Edison and Henry Ford said that many of their best ideas came to them while they exercised or during the relaxed period after completing exercise.

The last two chapters have been filled with benefits that we have received from walking and rebounding. We believe that many senior citizens will be blessed abundantly if they will establish an effective program of walking or another form of exercise. In the next chapter we will share with you some things we have learned about diet and the effect that a proper diet has on your health.

Chapter 24

The Hallelujah Diet

Now that we have shared our views on the relationship between an effective exercise program and a long and healthy life, we are ready to share our experience regarding diet, health and life expectancy. In this chapter we will give you information pertaining to the Hallelujah Diet.

Judy first became interested in similar principles to what the Hallelujah Diet teaches more than 50 years ago. Judy shared with me what she had learned. I joined her in changing my diet. In this chapter we will make available to you some amazing testimonies from people who have been helped by the Hallelujah Diet.

The Bible instructs us to not to tell anyone what to eat, when to eat or how to eat. We will merely share what we have learned. You then can decide if you are interested in all, part, or none of what we are sharing.

Judy sticks to the Hallelujah Diet very closely. I stick to it partially. We believe that you will be blessed by the information in this chapter, particularly the testimonies that we will give you and the numerous additional testimonies that you can find on the Hallelujah Diet website (see hacres.com).

The Hallelujah Diet originally was formulated by Rev. George Malkmus. Rev. Malkmus faced severe challenges with his health. He carefully studied the principles that today have evolved into the Hallelujah Diet. He was completely healed. He then began to share what he learned with others.

One of the basic concepts of Rev. Malkmus is that each church should have a health minister. Judy and I have completed the training to be health ministers. We became certified husband-wife health ministers (#289 in 1997) with Hallelujah Acres which is the organization that grew out of the original experiences that Rev. Malkmus had with the Hallelujah Diet. The words "Hallelujah Acres" refer to the property this organization owns in North Carolina.

More than 10,000 health ministers in the United States and in 57 foreign countries have been trained by Hallelujah Acres. More than 2,000,000 people are on the Hallelujah Diet.

More than 800 pastors have either attended health minister training or sent someone from their church to attend. You can attend a Health Minister Training at Hallelujah Acres, attend a Hallelujah Acres seminar in your area, or be trained online. See www.hacres.com. Hallelujah Acres has expanded their non-denominational Christian ministry into Canada, the United Kingdom, Europe, Australia and New Zealand.

There are many diets in the world today. As far as we know, no other diet even begins to approach the number of healing testimonies that you will find on the Hallelujah Acres website. You also can request their very interesting free weekly health tip by email.

One time I was talking on the telephone with a man who had been diagnosed with diabetes. He said that this condition caused him to wake up several times each night to go to the bathroom. The effects on his health had become so severe that he believed his life could be shortened by as much as 25 years by this disease.

I gave this man the website for the Hallelujah Diet. I suggested that he go there to look at testimonies regarding diabetes. He went to this website while we were talking on the phone. Suddenly he said, "I cannot believe what I am seeing. There must be at least 100 testimonies from people who have been helped with diabetes from this diet."

I told this man that some people might consider the Hallelujah Diet to be extreme. He said, "I don't care what I have to do. I am desperate."

On another occasion I was talking on the telephone to a friend who asked me to pray for a woman who had been diagnosed with breast cancer. I gave him the Hallelujah Acres website and suggested that he look for testimonies regarding breast cancer. This man also went to this website while we were talking.

He was very surprised to find more than 30 testimonies from women with breast cancer who had been helped by the Hallelujah Diet. I suggested that he pass this information on to the woman. He said that he would.

We believe you will be amazed by the tremendous number of testimonies from people all over the world whose health has dramatically improved as a result of the Hallelujah Diet. If you suffer from a specific illness, we recommend that you go to hacres.com to find testimonies in this specific area.

At the time that we wrote this chapter, we checked this website for testimonies in 4 areas – cancer, arthritis, heart disease and diabetes. We found 280 testimonies on cancer, 165 testimonies on arthritis and joint pain, 138 testimonies on heart health and 128 testimonies regarding diabetes.

Our purpose is NOT to attempt to explain the Hallelujah Diet in one short chapter. Doing this is impossible. Hacres.com will explain this information in detail. Our goal in this chapter has been to alert you to the amazing testimonies on this website.

We urge you *not* to begin by studying what the Hallelujah Diet is. If you are interested in the relationship between diet, healing and health, we believe that your interest will increase greatly after you study several testimonies from people who have experienced great improvement in their health. You then can decide whether you will study hacres.com for complete information on this diet and how it can affect your health.

The Hallelujah Diet derives its name from the many people who declared, "Hallelujah, I'm healed" after following this diet.

The Hallelujah Diet is a lifestyle. All of the food that God has created is included in this diet. Our prayer is that you will shout Hallelujah because you are healed and well and living a vibrant life. Our prayer is that you will prosper and be in good health (see III John 2).

Once again, the website is hacres.com. If you do not have access to the internet and you would like an in-depth explanation of the Hallelujah Diet, you can find this information in the book titled *The Hallelujah Diet* by George Malkmus.

Chapter 25

An Effective Method to Increase Your Energy

Now that we have shared some of our thoughts about exercise and diet, we would like to share some additional thoughts on the decrease in energy that many people experience as they grow older. This chapter will contain specific suggestions on dealing with this decreased energy.

I am 80 and Judy is 73 as this book goes to print. I believe that my energy level is above normal for a man my age, but my energy level cannot begin to compare with Judy's. The almost 8 year age difference could account for some of the difference, but I can tell you that Judy has an incredible energy level.

As I grow older, I often am conscious that my energy is significantly less than it was in the past. I am as mentally alert as ever. I know what God has called me to do with my life and I do it. However, as I face each day, I am continually conscious that I must utilize the energy that I have very carefully.

Although I am at an age where most people have retired, I am still very active writing books and in other aspects of Lamplight Ministries. I do not do this work to earn money. The monthly salary that Judy and I receive from Lamplight Ministries is very small in relation to the hours that we put in. I work diligently because I am certain that I am carrying out God's assignment for my life.

I have been a highly organized person for many years. My short-term "to do list" usually contains 20 to 30 items. My long-term list usually contains 80 to 100 items. I have similar lists now to what I had in the past, but I often have difficulty just completing my "have to have" items each week.

In the last two chapters we shared our thoughts on exercise and walking in particular. I have found that sticking to my exercise program is vitally important for me to have the energy that I require. Exercise is not optional for me. Daily exercise is mandatory. I cannot possibly carry out the assignment that God has given me without the energy that I receive from sticking to a regular exercise schedule.

When I write I am always conscious that God will give me supernatural energy to carry out His assignment. I like what the apostle Paul said when he said, "…I labor [unto weariness], striving with all the superhuman energy which He so mightily enkindles and works within me." (Colossians 1:29 AMP)

This verse and the amplification say that Paul "labored unto weariness." Anyone who has read Paul's writings extensively knows how committed Paul was to doing what God called him to do (see Acts 20:23-24). Paul knew that God gave him supernatural energy to complete his assignment.

I consistently experience this energy in my life. I thank God for this energy. Chapters 18, 19 and 20 in this book are devoted to seeking, finding, and carrying out God's will for your life. If you are totally committed to doing what God has called you to do, you *will* experience this supernatural energy from God.

There is a direct relationship between human energy and adequate sleep. God promises to bless His children with sleep. "…he giveth his beloved sleep." (Psalm 127:2 KJV)

Sleep is a gift from God. However, as we grow older, some of us need to learn how to receive this gift that our Father has made available to us. If you have problems sleeping, you might want to meditate on the following verse of Scripture. God said, "When you lie down, you shall not be afraid; yes, you shall lie down, and your sleep shall be sweet." (Proverbs 3:24 AMP)

Some younger people are able to get by without much sleep. The energy of youth sustains them. As many of us grow older, we understand how essential sleep is.

Sleep energizes you. Lack of sleep can affect your immune system. As I grow older, I have experienced problems getting enough sleep each night. I have found that daily naps are vitally important to me.

Before I share information on the importance of daily naps in my life, I want to emphasize that I understand that napping is not for everyone. I know some people who simply cannot take naps in the daytime.

I am just the opposite. I have been able to take naps for many years. I know that some of what I am about to say will seem extreme to people. All that I can tell you is what works for me. I pray that some people will find that the things I am sharing will be of benefit to them.

I do not believe I would be alive today if I had not taken thousands of naps during the past 35 years. I have been unable to get a good night's sleep for a long time. Naps are vital to me.

Many of my former business associates are deceased. Many of my high school and college classmates are deceased. Many of my friends and acquaintances who are younger than I am are suffering from severe health challenges.

My overall health is very good. I have not been to a doctor for more than 15 years for anything except a routine physical exam. I do not take any medication. I exercise consistently. I have lost more than 20 pounds in the last 10 years.

The *only* health challenge I have now and have had for many years is that my digestive system works less effectively with each passing year. I often am kept awake at night or awakened after I fall asleep by my stomach churning as it labors to digest food.

I normally get between three and four hours of sleep at night. I do a lot of my writing when I am awake during the night. However, the only way that I can consistently exceed my writing goals is by taking several naps each day.

I put out a lot of energy for someone my age. There is *no* way that I could do the tremendous amount of writing and the other work that I do for Lamplight Ministries at the age of 80 without taking naps. I am very grateful for naps. Naps have enabled me to carry out God's assignment for many years when I could not do this otherwise.

I understand that naps are impractical for some people who are reading this book. If you are working five or more days a week, you often will not be able to fit a nap into your schedule except on weekends.

I never thought about taking naps until I was in my forties. I received tremendous benefit from naps when I flew to different areas in the United States and Canada to give seminars on *Trust God for Your Finances*. I especially remember one seminar that I gave in Vancouver, British Columbia, in Canada when I was 55 years old. I can remember taking naps as I flew across the United States and Canada. I fell asleep several times on that flight. I was amazed at how refreshed I was when I arrived in Vancouver.

On shorter flights I often took as many as two or three short naps. As soon as the seat belt sign went off, I reclined my seat as far as it would go. I napped just as I sometimes do in the recliner in our living room.

I occasionally took naps in my office when I was a businessman in New Hampshire. When I knew that I needed a break, I told my secretary that I did not want to be disturbed for a specific amount of time – usually 15 to 30 minutes. I closed the door and relaxed in my desk chair. Sometimes I was able to briefly drop off to sleep. Other times I just rested. I used to keep a small alarm clock in my office for these naps. I always was refreshed after these short naps whether I slept or not.

Judy and I now work out of our home. Lamplight Ministries does not have office space. We have a small warehouse where we store our publications. Books and Scripture cards are shipped from there. Judy and I do our Lamplight Ministries work out of two bedrooms at opposite ends of our home.

For many years I have turned off my telephone and allowed the answering machine to take messages while I napped. When I expend a burst of energy, usually after writing for awhile, I write until I am tired. I then take a short nap. I wake up refreshed and ready for another spurt of writing.

Because I have been interested in naps for many years, I have studied the lives of many successful people who took naps. When Winston Churchill was the prime minister of Great Britain, he took a nap almost every afternoon.

Mr. Churchill was 66 years old when he took office in 1940. At an age when many people had retired, he amazed people with his ability to work long hours leading his country under extreme pressure during World War II.

Mr. Churchill attributed much of this ability to the fact that he often spent one or two hours in bed each day after lunch. He completely undressed, put on pajamas and went to sleep just as he did at night. He then started his day all over again in the middle of the afternoon and was able to work into the evening. Mr. Churchill once said, "Don't think that you will be doing less work because you sleep during the day. That is a foolish notion held by people who have no imagination. You will accomplish more. You will do one-and-a-half to two days of work in one."

Roger Babson was a successful Christian businessman who often was called upon by government leaders for advice. Mr. Babson once said, "As soon as possible after lunch each day I take a brief nap, after which I have a quiet twenty minutes in private worship. The busier my day and the greater my responsibilities, the more particular I am to have this quiet period. I try to read a little Scripture, pray a short prayer and then spend a few minutes in meditation. Faith and power have come to me during these short daily quiet periods. I earnestly recommend them."

Both Prime Minister Churchill and Mr. Babson spoke of taking naps after lunch. John D. Rockefeller, who lived to the age of 98, said that one of the reasons he lived so long was because he took a 30-minute nap after lunch each day.[1]

The British novelist, Somerset Maugham, also was extremely productive at an advanced age. Mr. Maugham wrote books until his early nineties. He attributed his vitality to the nap that he took after lunch each day.

I mentioned Thomas Edison in a previous chapter. Many people who have studied his life have attributed his creativity and his tremendous endurance to the naps that he often took. Mr. Edison did most his inventions at his laboratory in Menlo Park, New Jersey. He had a couch in his office where he often napped.

Mr. Edison only slept an average of four hours a night. He once said, "Just sleep four hours and get up. In a little while the feeling of fatigue will pass and you won't want to sleep any more. Sleeping only four hours makes the sleep much deeper."

Mr. Edison was able to put in many productive hours each week because he often took naps in his office. His wife once said, "He could work hard and long, then lie on his old couch and go immediately to sleep."

Bob Hope was a well-known Hollywood entertainer. He lived into his 90s. Mr. Hope told reporters that his energy came as a result of the naps that he often took between performances and when he was flying on an airplane.

Connie Mack was a successful major league baseball manager in the first half of the 20th century. He was very active into his 90s. Mr. Mack attributed his energy at an advanced age to the nap that he always took before managing a game.

Many presidents of the United States have emphasized that naps have helped them to discharge the awesome responsibilities of that office. Warren G. Harding often took naps in the Oval Office. Calvin Coolidge took a nap each afternoon. Presidents Ronald Reagan and Bill Clinton have been reported to have taken daytime naps while they were in office. Many of these men were in their 60s and 70s.

Fatigue can be a significant problem as you grow older. Vince Lombardi was a Super Bowl championship football coach with the Green Bay Packers. Coach Lombardi once said, "Fatigue makes cowards of us all." Most of us know from experience that problems often seem to be much worse than they actually are when we are tired.

Daily naps are a normal part of everyday life in many South American and Mediterranean countries. In some of these countries, the law requires every business establishment to close from noon until 2:00 p.m. each afternoon. Many of the people in these countries take naps during this time.

Some people are like cats. Cats do not require sustained periods of sleep. They function better when they get their rest in short segments. Cats usually are awake a great deal during the night and take several naps during the day. This sleep pattern is normal for cats. This is where the expression "cat naps" comes from.

I keep careful records as to how much sleep I get each night and how much nap time I get each day. I have kept these records for more than 20 years. I keep taking naps each day until I reach a minimum of 6 hours of sleep in a 24-hour period.

I hope that the information in this chapter has been helpful to you. The last 6 chapters of this book have not contained as much Scripture as the first 19 chapters. In these chapters we have shared many things from our personal experience that we hope will help you as you grow older.

In the next chapter we will look into the Word of God to see what it says about not being afraid of death. Many older people are afraid of death. We pray that the following information from the Word of God will help you if you are afraid of death.

Chapter 26

You Should Not Be Afraid of Death

Your Father is very interested in your death. "Precious (important and no light matter) in the sight of the Lord is the death of His saints (His loving ones)." (Psalm 116:15 AMP)

If Jesus Christ is your Savior, you are a saint in the eyes of God because Jesus paid the full price for all of your sins. Your death is very important to God.

Your Father does not want you to be afraid of death. You should be like the psalmist David who said, "…though I walk through the [deep, sunless] valley of the shadow of death, I will fear or dread no evil, for You are with me; Your rod [to protect] and Your staff [to guide], they comfort me." (Psalm 23:4 AMP)

This verse of Scripture that is read at many Christian funerals applies to your life. The Bible refers to your death as a shadow. Visualize a shadow under a tree. This shadow has no substance. Death has no substance in the eternal realm. Death is compared to a valley that you walk *through*.

Your Father assures you that He *will* be with you when you go through the valley of death. This valley is between earth and heaven. God will protect you, guide you and comfort you when you go through this valley.

Jesus has paid the full price to set you free from the fear of death. "…by [going through] death He might bring to nought and make of no effect him who had the power of death – that is, the devil – and also that He might deliver and completely set free all those who through the [haunting] fear of death were held in bondage throughout the whole course of their lives." (Hebrews 2:14-15 AMP)

Jesus went through death for you. The power of death that Satan has over unbelievers is nullified in your life if Jesus Christ is your Savior. Do not give Satan and his demons power that they do not have. Jesus has *"delivered* you and set you *completely free* from the [haunting] fear of death."

The word "haunting" that is used in the amplification of this verse refers to Satan. This word is used in the same context as describing a so-called haunted house. When a house is called haunted, it supposedly is filled with ghosts. Do not allow Satan's demons to haunt you by their attempts to hold you in bondage through fear of death. If you will consistently study and meditate on this verse and the other verses of Scripture that are contained in this chapter, you will *not* fear death.

Fear of death is primarily caused by fear of the unknown. Any Christian who fears death either does not know what God's Word says about death or does not have absolute faith that what God's Word says about death is true.

Jesus took the keys of death away from Satan. Jesus said, "…Do not be afraid! I am the First and the Last, and the Everliving One [I am living in the eternity of the eternities]. I died, but see, I am alive forevermore; and I possess the keys of death and Hades (the realm of the dead)." (Revelation 1:17-18 AMP)

Once again, you are told that you should *not* be afraid of death. Before Jesus rose from the dead, He went to Hades and took the keys of death away from Satan. Hades was the place where dead people went before Jesus rose from death.

The prophet Isaiah prophesied that Jesus would win a glorious victory over death. More than 700 years before Jesus rose from the dead, Isaiah said, "He will swallow up death [in victory; He will abolish death forever]…." (Isaiah 25:8 AMP)

Jesus won a glorious victory over death when He rose from the grave. The New Testament tells you that this Old Testament prophesy made by Isaiah was fulfilled. "...when this perishable puts on the imperishable and this that was capable of dying puts on freedom from death, then shall be fulfilled the Scripture that says, Death is swallowed up (utterly vanquished forever) in and unto victory. O death, where is your victory? O death, where is your sting?" (I Corinthians 15:54-55 AMP)

When Christian believers die, they exchange their perishable earthly bodies for an imperishable heavenly body. If Jesus Christ is your Savior, death has *no* victory over you. The sting was taken out of death when you received Jesus as your Savior. You can be certain that Jesus has destroyed the power of death in the life of every person who has received Him as his or her Savior.

When Jesus rose from the dead, He won the greatest victory of all time. The Bible speaks of "...our Savior Christ Jesus, Who annulled death and made it of no effect and brought life and immortality (immunity from eternal death) to light..." (II Timothy 1:10 AMP)

When something is annulled, it is cancelled, done away with and invalidated. If Jesus Christ is your Savior, the incredible victory that He won has made death *of no effect* in your life. "...the [consistently] righteous has hope and confidence even in death." (Proverbs 14:32 AMP)

The words "the consistently righteous" in this verse and the amplification refer to the righteousness that you have before God if Jesus Christ is your Savior. These words also refer to you doing your very best to consistently live a righteous life by learning and obeying God's instructions in the Bible. If you do this, you will be confident when you face death.

The death of a Christian is a time of triumph, not a time of defeat. If Jesus Christ is your Savior, death will take you *out* of the darkness of a world that is dominated by Satan and his demons into the light of a world that is dominated by Jesus Christ (see John 8:12, Ephesians 5:8 and I Peter 2:9).

God's perspective pertaining to death is very different from the perspective of unbelievers. You should look at death as the apostle Paul did when he said, "...to die is gain [the gain of the glory of eternity]." (Philippians 1:21 AMP)

Death is gain, not loss. Death is good, not bad. Death seems bad to unbelievers who do not understand what the Bible teaches about death.

When you die, your body dies. Your spirit does not die. The day that you die is your graduation day. This is the day when you graduate from your life on earth to a glorious new life in heaven.

God's ways are much higher and very different from the ways of the world (see Isaiah 55:8-9). Death is your friend, not your enemy. When Jesus rose from the dead, He made it possible for every person who has received Him as his or her Savior to live throughout eternity with Him in the glory of heaven. Jesus said, "...because I live, you will live also." (John 14:19 AMP)

Do not look at death as a departure. Look at death as an *arrival*. The tears that are shed when a Christian dies actually are tears for the person who is crying.

You should be filled with anticipation if you are growing older and you know that death is drawing near. If you know that death is approaching, heaven should fill your thoughts. We recommend our book, *What Will Heaven Be Like?*. This book is filled with Scripture that describes what the Bible says about heaven. In the next two chapters we will take a brief look at heaven. These chapters will summarize much, but not all, of the Scripture that is contained in *What Will Heaven Be Like?*.

Chapter 27

Every Christian Is a Citizen of Heaven

You have seen that the Bible instructs you not to be afraid of death. In the next two chapters you will learn why God says that you should not fear death. If you have received Jesus Christ as your Savior, you will be "...[born anew] into an inheritance which is beyond the reach of change and decay [imperishable], unsullied and unfading, reserved in heaven for you." (I Peter 1:4 AMP)

Most people on earth rejoice when they receive an inheritance. If Jesus is your Savior, you will be "born anew into an *inheritance* which is beyond the reach of change and decay." God will give you a magnificent new beginning in the glorious place He has reserved for you in heaven. If Jesus is your Savior, your name is written in the Lamb's Book of Life (see Revelation 21:27). Jesus said, "...rejoice that your names are enrolled in heaven." (Luke 10:20 AMP)

You should rejoice as you read the magnificent scriptural truths in these two chapters about the glory of heaven. If you are not absolutely *certain* that you will live throughout eternity in heaven, please turn to the Appendix at the end of this book. This Appendix contains specific instructions that explain what God instructs you to do to be absolutely certain that you will live in heaven throughout eternity.

If Jesus is your Savior, your present home on earth is only a temporary home. When you arrive in heaven, you will have arrived at your *real home*. "...we are citizens of the state (commonwealth, homeland) which is in heaven..." (Philippians 3:20 AMP)

You are listed as a citizen of the country where you live on earth. However, if Jesus is your Savior, God has you listed as a citizen of heaven. You are just passing through this world. You will live in the glory of heaven throughout eternity.

You are a citizen of heaven *now* if Jesus is your Savior. You do not have to wait until you arrive in heaven to become a citizen of heaven. You truly will be going home when you go to heaven. "...consider and look not to the things that are seen but to the things that are unseen; for the things that are visible are temporal (brief and fleeting), but the things that are invisible are deathless and everlasting." (II Corinthians 4:18 AMP)

The Word of God says that you should *not* focus on things that you can see. Instead of focusing on the things of the world that you can see with your human eyesight, you are instructed to focus on "the things that are unseen." Everything in the world is temporary. Everything in heaven is eternal.

As you learn more about the glory of heaven, your life will not revolve around the things of this world. You will focus on the glorious eternal life that awaits you in heaven. "...set your minds and keep them set on what is above (the higher things), not on the things that are on the earth. For [as far as this world is concerned] you have died, and your [new, real] life is hidden with Christ in God." (Colossians 3:2-3 AMP)

Once again you are instructed to focus on heaven, *not* on things that are on earth. As you grow older and your time on earth grows shorter, you should learn, understand and meditate on these awesome scriptural truths pertaining to heaven. "...Eye hath not seen, nor ear heard, neither have entered into the heart of man, the things which God hath prepared for them that love him." (I Corinthians 2:9 KJV)

Your eyes have never seen anything on earth that can remotely compare with the glory of heaven. Your ears have never heard anything on earth that can compare with the magnificence of what you will hear in heaven.

Please stop for a minute to think of the most beautiful place you have ever seen on earth. The beauty of heaven far exceeds the beauty of the most delightful place you have seen on earth. Think of the most beautiful music you have ever heard. The music in heaven is far superior to the most magnificent music you have heard on earth. You cannot begin to comprehend with the limitations of your human understanding how glorious and magnificent heaven is.

There is no such thing as night in heaven. "...there shall be no more night; they have no need for lamplight or sunlight, for the Lord God will illuminate them and be their light..." (Revelation 22:5 AMP)

You will never see darkness again after you leave the earth. God illuminates heaven. Heaven is filled with God's glorious light at all times. You will be aware of this supernatural light from the first moment you arrive in heaven.

There are no cloudy, gray and gloomy days in heaven. There is no rain or snow in heaven. Heaven is filled with the glorious light of God at all times.

Your heart will sing with joy when you are in heaven. "...the ransomed of the Lord shall return and come to Zion with singing, and everlasting joy shall be upon their heads..." (Isaiah 35:10 AMP)

The happiest day that you have ever experienced during your life on earth cannot remotely compare with the joy that you will experience throughout eternity in heaven. Everyone in heaven is continually filled with the joy of the Lord.

Heaven is the eternal home of God. Heaven is the eternal home of Jesus Christ. Because heaven is the home of God and the home of Jesus, you can be absolutely certain that heaven is a glorious place. Only God could conceive the eternal paradise that He has prepared for His beloved children.

You will see Jesus Christ face to face when you arrive in heaven. You cannot comprehend how you will feel when you stand before Jesus and see Him in all of His glory. "...we shall see Him just as He [really] is." (I John 3:2 AMP)

You may wonder what Jesus looks like. You will never wonder again because you will have the opportunity to see for yourself. "Your eyes will see the King in His beauty..." (Isaiah 33:17 AMP)

We have explained that you have an assignment to complete for God here on earth. You should focus on completing this assignment, but you also should look forward to heaven as the apostle Paul did when he said, "...My yearning desire is to depart (to be free of this world, to set forth) and be with Christ..." (Philippians 1:23 AMP)

Paul yearned to leave this world to be with Jesus throughout eternity. The Holy Spirit revealed the glory of heaven to Paul. As the Holy Spirit reveals great spiritual truths to you as you read the Scripture in these two chapters, we believe that you also will yearn for the magnificence of heaven that awaits you. "...always (through the eternity of the eternities) we shall be with the Lord! Therefore comfort and encourage one another with these words." (I Thessalonians 4:17-18 AMP)

You will only be on earth for a relatively short time. You will live eternally with Jesus in heaven. You should be greatly comforted and encouraged by the glorious scriptural truths you have read in these chapters.

Jesus is the center of attraction in heaven. When you see Jesus face to face in all of His glory, you will not be able to take your eyes off Him. You will be filled with awe and reverence.

We believe that you will be able to see the scars on His body. Jesus will be the only person in heaven with scars on His body. These scars are heavenly evidence of the supreme sacrifice that Jesus made for you during His earthly ministry.

You will be able to enjoy continual intimate fellowship with Jesus in heaven. Do not make the mistake of thinking that Jesus will be so busy that He will not be able to find time for you. We now will look again at a verse of Scripture that we studied in Chapter 11. God is able to sit on His throne in heaven and, at the same time, to live in the heart of *every* one of the billions of people on earth at the *same* time. "One God and Father of [us] all, Who is above all [Sovereign over all], pervading all and [living] in [us] all." (Ephesians 4:6 AMP)

God is omnipresent. Jesus also is omnipresent. He is fully able to have an intimate conversation with every person in heaven at the same time. You will be able to enjoy a close and intimate personal relationship with Jesus throughout eternity in heaven.

In this chapter we have explained great truths pertaining to the glory of heaven and your ability to see Jesus Christ when you are in heaven. In the next chapter we will look into God's Word for additional instruction about the supernatural health that you will enjoy in heaven, the warm and intimate relationships that you will enjoy with other people in heaven and the rewards that you will receive in heaven for your service to God during your life on earth.

Chapter 28

There Is No Pain or Sorrow in Heaven

The Bible teaches that every person in heaven is very happy. There are no sad people in heaven. "God will wipe away every tear from their eyes; and death shall be no more, neither shall there be anguish (sorrow and mourning) nor grief nor pain any more, for the old conditions and the former order of things have passed away." (Revelation 21:4 AMP)

There will be no tears in heaven. There will be no death in heaven. There will be no sorrow in heaven. Pain will disappear. Everything on earth that caused problems of any kind will disappear when you are in heaven. You will be problem-free and pain-free throughout eternity.

When you take your last breath, your spirit is immediately in the presence of Jesus Christ (see II Corinthians 5:8). Your body remains wherever it was buried. If you were cremated, your ashes are still your body. If your ashes were scattered at sea and have been absorbed into the ocean or if your body was burned, your body will suddenly reappear in a new heavenly form at the moment the trumpet is sounded (see I Corinthians 15:52 and I Thessalonians 4:16). Those who died in Christ will rise up out of the grave to join Christ Jesus in the air. Then the believers on earth will rise into the air to join the Lord.

The Bible teaches that you will receive a glorious new body in heaven. Your earthly body, with any aches and pains that you might have had, will not go to heaven. "There are heavenly bodies (sun, moon, and stars) and there are earthly bodies (men, animals, and plants), but the beauty and glory of the heavenly bodies is of one kind, while the beauty and glory of earthly bodies is a different kind." (I Corinthians 15:40 AMP)

Your heavenly body will be far superior to your earthly body, no matter how good your physical condition may be. "…[The body] that is sown is perishable and decays, but [the body] that is resurrected is imperishable (immune to decay, immortal). It is sown in dishonor and humiliation; it is raised in honor and glory. It is sown in infirmity and weakness; it is resurrected in strength and endued with power." (I Corinthians 15:42-43 AMP)

We studied II Corinthians 4:16 in Chapter 2. This verse of Scripture speaks of the progressive decay that many people on earth experience in their bodies as they grow older. I Corinthians 15:42 also speaks of the decay of earthly bodies. It goes on to say that your heavenly body is "imperishable, immune to decay." There will be no decay in your heavenly body which will be filled with supernatural strength and power.

You have so much to look forward to with the glorious new body you will have in heaven. "…we know that if the tent which is our earthly home is destroyed (dissolved), we have from God a building, a house not made with hands, eternal in the heavens." (II Corinthians 5:1 AMP)

Your earthly body is described as a tent. A tent is a temporary dwelling place. Your earthly body will be destroyed because of the heavenly body that you will receive from God. Instead of being a tent, your heavenly body is referred to as "a house not made with hands." "…in this [present abode, body], we sigh and groan inwardly, because we yearn to be clothed over [we yearn to put on our celestial body like a garment, to be fitted out] with our heavenly dwelling" (II Corinthians 5:2 AMP)

You may struggle because of discomfort in your body here on earth. Your heavenly body will be incredibly healthy. You did not earn and you do not deserve the glorious supernatural body that you will enjoy when you are in heaven. Your loving Father will provide this tremendous body for you through His grace because of the supreme sacrifice that Jesus made for you when He died on the cross at Calvary.

Your physical condition in heaven will be far superior to the physical condition of the most superbly conditioned human being who ever lived on earth. Everyone in heaven enjoys perfect health.

There is no fatigue in heaven. There are no doctors, nurses or hospitals. There are no pharmacies or prescriptions. There are no funerals or funeral homes. There are no cemeteries in heaven.

In addition to a perfect body in heaven, you also will be perfect mentally and emotionally. No one in heaven is selfish. Every person in heaven is selfless and loving. The Bible speaks of "...the spirits of the righteous (the redeemed in heaven) who have been made perfect." (Hebrews 12:23 AMP)

You are righteous before God if Jesus Christ is your Savior. You have been redeemed. Your spirit will be made perfect in heaven. Every person in heaven is cleansed of all of his or her earthly imperfections.

Any problem that you might have experienced in your relationship with other people on earth will no longer exist in heaven. Every person in heaven reaches out to every other person with humble, unconditional and selfless love. "There shall no longer exist there anything that is accursed (detestable, foul, offensive, impure, hateful, or horrible)...." (Revelation 22:3 AMP)

Nothing in heaven is evil or negative in any way. You will not remember anything bad that may have happened in your life on earth. God will supernaturally erase all earthly problems from your consciousness when you are in heaven. He said, "...I create new heavens and a new earth. And the former things shall not be remembered or come into mind." (Isaiah 65:17 AMP)

Everything in heaven will be fresh and new. The atmosphere in heaven is incredible. You cannot begin to comprehend how glorious heaven is.

Can you think of one sin on earth that is not caused by selfishness? *Every* sin is rooted in selfishness. There is no selfishness in heaven. No one is self-seeking or self-centered.

No one in heaven criticizes other people. There are no disagreements or arguments in heaven. Every relationship that every person in heaven has with every other person is supernaturally perfect.

There is no anger in heaven. No one in heaven is envious or jealous. Every person in heaven wants the very best for every other person in heaven because every person in heaven has been cleansed so that he or she will put God first, other people second and themselves last.

If members of your family received Jesus Christ as their Savior on earth, you will experience an incredible family reunion when you arrive in heaven. Your loved ones will have many glorious experiences to share with you.

You will see loved ones in heaven who were in failing health when you last saw them on earth. These people will be in robust good health. You will rejoice to see how well your loved ones are doing in their new lives in heaven.

In addition to the glorious reunion with other members of your family, you also will see many Christian friends who preceded you to heaven. You will re-establish warm and intimate relationships with these people that will continue throughout eternity. You also will establish wonderful new relationships with other Christians in heaven. The richness of fellowship in heaven will be far beyond anything that you can begin to comprehend.

No one in heaven is lonely because there are no surface relationships in heaven. Every person in heaven has a close and intimate relationship with every other person.

Also, everything that you did not understand during your life on earth will be revealed to you in heaven. "…we are looking in a mirror that gives only a dim (blurred) reflection [of reality as in a riddle or enigma], but then [when perfection comes] we shall see in reality and face to face! Now I know in part (imperfectly), but then I shall know and understand fully and clearly, even in the same manner as I have been fully and clearly known and understood [by God]." (I Corinthians 13:12 AMP)

Your understanding on earth is compared to something that you cannot see clearly when you look into a mirror. In heaven you will see everything as it really is. You will see God face to face. You will completely understand many things that you did not understand on earth.

Most people on earth think in terms of the 70, 80, 90 or even 100 years that they hope to live. The relatively short lifespan of people on earth cannot begin to compare with living throughout eternity in heaven. Someone once said that the amount of time you will spend on earth can be compared to one tiny grain of sand on the largest beach in the world. All of the grains of sand together on the largest beach in the world will give you an understanding of eternity in heaven compared to the very brief time you will live on earth.

There are no clocks in heaven. No one in heaven rushes. Everything in heaven is permanent. Nothing wears out or goes out of style.

Think of the most wonderful vacation you ever enjoyed here on earth. No vacation on earth, no matter how enjoyable it may have been, can remotely compare with the glorious rest that every Christian will experience throughout eternity in heaven.

In Chapters 17, 18 and 19 we studied several verses of Scripture that explained the specific assignment that God has for every person on earth. You will be rewarded in heaven for completing the assignment God has given to you. "...for whatever good anyone does, he will receive his reward from the Lord..." (Ephesians 6:8 AMP)

The Lord will reward you for everything you have done to serve Him on earth. "...Blessed (happy, to be envied) are the dead from now on who die in the Lord! Yes, blessed (happy, to be envied indeed), says the Spirit, [in] that they may rest from their labors, for their works (deeds) do follow (attend, accompany) them!" (Revelation 14:13 AMP)

You will be blessed incredibly when you are in heaven. Your work on earth has been completed. You will rest from your labor. Your good work on earth will be recognized in heaven. God knows exactly what you did to carry out His assignment. He will reward you for your faithfulness. You will be humble and grateful.

If you were persecuted for your Christian beliefs during your life on earth, you will be rewarded in heaven. Jesus said, "Blessed (happy, to be envied, and spiritually prosperous – with life-joy and satisfaction in God's favor and salvation, regardless of your outward conditions) are you when people revile you and persecute you and say all kinds of evil things against you falsely on My account. Be glad and supremely joyful, for your reward in heaven is great (strong and intense)..." (Matthew 5:11-12 AMP)

You will be blessed for the times that people on earth persecuted you because of your Christian beliefs. You are told that you should be glad when people persecute you on earth because of the wonderful reward you will receive in heaven.

With every day that passes, you are one day closer to your magnificent eternal home in heaven. Your future is incredible. Thank You, dear Father. Thank You, Lord Jesus.

Conclusion

This book contains many scriptural instructions that will help you to live the final years of your life on earth the way that God wants you to live. If you learn and faithfully obey these specific instructions from God, the final years of your life will be full, balanced and complete.

You have learned that your Father instructs you to renew your mind by studying His Word each day as you grow older. If you have not highlighted or underlined specific passages of Scripture as you read this book, we advise you to go back now and read the book again. Highlight or underline anything in the book that you want to be able to refer to in the future. Write notes in the margins. When you do this, you will be renewing your mind. You also will have provided yourself with selected verses of Scripture to meditate on day and night.

Please pray about sharing a copy of this book with your friends and loved ones. You can help other people to increase the effectiveness of their final years by making this specific information from the Word of God available to them.

The prices of our books are as low as we can make them. We also offer quantity discounts. The order form in the back of this book explains our discounts. We desire to help as many people with the Word of God as we possibly can.

If this book has helped you, would you share your testimony with us? We normally need three or four paragraphs in a testimony to consolidate them into a one paragraph testimony for our newsletter and our website. Your comments will encourage many people, including the inmates in prisons and jails and people in Third World countries who receive our publications free of charge.

Please send any comments to lamplightmin@yahoo.com. You also can mail your comments to Jack and Judy Hartman at PO Box 1307, Dunedin, Florida 34697. You can call 1-800-540-1597 and leave a message for Judy.

We invite you to visit our website: www.lamplight.net. You will find a section on biblical health as well as recipes that Judy adds each month to bless you. I (Jack) would not be alive today if it were not for Judy's knowledge and wisdom regarding biblical health and her delicious recipes.

We have been blessed to share with you the results of the many hours of effort we have invested to learn what the Bible says about the final years of your life on earth and your eternal life in heaven. Your letting us know if this book has made a difference means so much to us. We are looking forward to hearing from you. We are praying for you. We love you.

Blessed to be a blessing (Genesis 12:1-3)

Jack and Judy

Appendix

This book is filled with instructions and promises from God. However, if you have not received Jesus Christ as your Savior, you *cannot understand* the scriptural truths that are contained in this book. "…the mind of the flesh [with its carnal thoughts and purposes] is hostile to God, for it does not submit itself to God's Law; indeed it cannot." (Romans 8:7 AMP)

Please notice the word "cannot" in this verse of Scripture. If Jesus is not your Savior, you cannot understand and obey God's instructions.

People who have not received Jesus Christ as their Savior are not open to the specific instructions that God has given to us in the Bible. "…the natural, nonspiritual man does not accept or welcome or admit into his heart the gifts and teachings and revelations of the Spirit of God, for they are folly (meaningless nonsense) to him; and he is incapable of knowing them [of progressively recognizing, understanding, and becoming better acquainted with them] because they are spiritually discerned and estimated and appreciated." (I Corinthians 2:14 AMP)

The words "does not accept or welcome or admit into his heart the gifts and teachings and revelations of the Spirit of God" in this verse of Scripture are very important. Some people are strongly opposed to the Bible and what it teaches. They look at Scripture references from the Bible as "meaningless nonsense." These people are incapable of learning great spiritual truths from God until and unless they receive Jesus Christ as their Savior.

At the close of this Appendix we will explain exactly what you should do to receive Jesus Christ as your Savior. If and when you make this decision, the glorious supernatural truths of the Bible will open up to you. Jesus said, "...To you it has been given to know the secrets and mysteries of the kingdom of heaven, but to them it has not been given." (Matthew 13:11 AMP)

Jesus was speaking to *you* when He said that you can "know the secrets and mysteries of the kingdom of heaven." You must not miss out on the glorious privilege that is available to every believer to know and understand the ways of God.

A spiritual veil blocks all unbelievers from understanding the things of God. "...even if our Gospel (the glad tidings) also be hidden (obscured and covered up with a veil that hinders the knowledge of God), it is hidden [only] to those who are perishing and obscured [only] to those who are spiritually dying and veiled [only] to those who are lost." (II Corinthians 4:3 AMP)

When and if you receive Jesus Christ as your Savior, this spiritual veil is pulled aside. "...whenever a person turns [in repentance] to the Lord, the veil is stripped off and taken away." (II Corinthians 3:16 AMP)

If you obey the scriptural instructions at the end of this Appendix, Jesus Christ will become your Savior. Everything in your life will become fresh and new. "...if any person is [ingrafted] in Christ (the Messiah) he is a new creation (a new creature altogether); the old [previous moral and spiritual condition] has passed away. Behold, the fresh and new has come!" (II Corinthians 5:17 AMP)

Instead of being opposed to the teachings of the holy Bible, you will be completely open to these teachings. You will have a hunger and thirst to continually learn more supernatural truths from the Word of God. "...I endorse and delight in the Law of God in my inmost self [with my new nature]." (Romans 7:22 AMP)

Every person who has not received Jesus Christ as his or her Savior is a sinner who is doomed to live throughout eternity in the horror of hell. God has made it possible for *you* to escape this terrible eternal penalty. "...God so loved the world, that he gave his only begotten Son, that whosoever believeth in him should not perish, but have everlasting life." (John 3:16 KJV)

God knew that everyone who lived on earth after Adam and Eve would be a sinner because of the sins of Adam and Eve (see Romans 3:10-12). He sent His only Son to take upon Himself the sins of the world as He died a horrible death by crucifixion. If you believe that Jesus Christ paid the full price for *your* sins and if you trust Him completely for your eternal salvation, you will live with Him eternally in the glory of heaven.

There is only *one* way for you to live eternally in heaven after you die – that is to receive eternal salvation through Jesus Christ. "Jesus saith unto him, I am the way, the truth, and the life: no man cometh unto the Father, but by me." (John 14:6 KJV)

If you trust in anyone or anything except Jesus Christ for your eternal salvation, you will not live eternally in heaven. If you are reading these truths about living eternally in heaven because of the price that Jesus Christ has paid for you, you must understand that the same God Who created you actually is drawing you to come to Jesus Christ for eternal salvation. Jesus said, "No one is able to come to Me unless the Father Who sent Me attracts and draws him and gives him the desire to come to Me…" (John 6:44 AMP)

Are you interested in these spiritual truths about where you will live throughout eternity? If you are, you can be certain that the same awesome God Who created you is drawing *you* to Jesus Christ at this very moment.

Heaven is a glorious place. Everyone in heaven is perfectly healthy and very happy. "…God shall wipe away all tears from their eyes; and there shall be no more death, neither sorrow, nor crying, neither shall there be any more pain: for the former things are passed away. (Revelation 21:4 KJV)

All of the problems of earth will disappear when you arrive in heaven. No one in heaven dies. No one in heaven is sad. No one in heaven cries. No one in heaven suffers from pain.

You will live eternally in one place or another when you die. If you do not receive Jesus Christ as your Savior, you will live eternally in hell. People in hell will experience continual torment throughout eternity. "...the smoke of their torment ascendeth up for ever and ever: and they have no rest day nor night..." (Revelation 14:11 KJV)

Everyone in heaven is filled with joy. Everyone in hell is miserable. Jesus described what hell would be like when He said, "...there will be weeping and wailing and grinding of teeth. (Matthew 13:42 AMP)

Throughout eternity the inhabitants of hell will weep and wail. They will grind their teeth in anguish. Can you imagine living this way for the endless trillions of years of eternity? This is exactly what will happen to *you* if you reject Jesus Christ as your Savior.

How do you receive eternal salvation through Jesus Christ? "...if you acknowledge and confess with your lips that Jesus is Lord and in your heart believe (adhere to, trust in, and rely on the truth) that God raised Him from the dead, you will be saved. For with the heart a person believes (adheres to, trusts in, and relies on Christ) and so is justified (declared righteous, acceptable to God), and with the mouth he confesses (declares openly and speaks out freely his faith) and confirms [his] salvation." (Romans 10:9-10 AMP)

You must *believe in your heart* (not just think in your mind) that Jesus paid the full price for all of your sins when He was crucified. You must believe that God raised Jesus from the dead. You must open your mouth and *speak this truth* that you believe in your heart. If you believe in your heart that Jesus Christ died and rose again from the dead and that the price for your sins has been paid for and you tell others that you believe this great spiritual truth, you *have* been saved. You *will* live eternally in heaven.

If Jesus Christ was not your Savior when you began to read this book, we pray that He is your Savior now. Your life will change immensely. You will never be the same again. Every aspect of your life will be gloriously new.

Please let us know if you have become a child of God by receiving eternal salvation through Jesus Christ. We would like to pray for you and welcome you as our new Christian brother or sister. We love you and bless you in the name of our Lord Jesus Christ.

We would be so pleased to hear from you. If you are already a believer, we would be pleased to hear from you as well. We invite you to visit our website at www.lamplight.net. Please let us know if this book or one or more of our other publications has made a difference in our life. Please give us your comments so that we can share these comments in our newsletters and on our website to encourage other people.

Study Guide

What Did You Learn From This Book?

The questions in this Study Guide are carefully arranged to show you how much you have learned about God's Instructions for growing older. This Study Guide is not intended to be an academic test. The sole purpose of the following questions is to help you increase your practical knowledge pertaining to God's instructions for growing older.

Page Reference

1. God promises to carry you from your birth to your old age when your hair is white. How can you use this passage of Scripture if you are an older person and you are struggling in any way? How do some older people block God from carrying out this promise? (Isaiah 46:3-4) 31

2. What does the Bible say is the normal lifespan of a human being? (Psalm 90:10) 32

3. How old was Moses when he died? How good was his health during the final years of his life? (Deuteronomy 4:7) 32

4. How can you be certain that God's promise to carry you throughout your life is completely reliable? (I Corinthians 1:9) 33

5. What two things are you instructed to do to live a long

	life? (Proverbs 4:10) 33
6.	What two things are you instructed to do to receive supernatural tranquility from God throughout your old age until the time that you die? (Proverbs 3:1-2) 33
7.	What additional instructions are you given that will enable you to receive long life? (Deuteronomy 30:20, Proverbs 9:11 and Proverbs 10:27) 34
8.	What does the Bible instruct you to do if your body is decaying? (II Corinthians 4:16) 35
9.	What does the Bible refer to when it speaks of your inner self? (I Peter 3:4) 36
10.	What are you instructed to do with your old unrenewed self? How frequently are you instructed to renew your mind in the Word of God? (Ephesians 4:22-24) 36
11.	What are you instructed to do so that you will not conform to the external, superficial customs of the world? How will your life change if you obey this instruction from the Word of God? (Romans 12:2) 37
12.	The Bible speaks of the wisdom and understanding that some older people have. How do you receive supernatural wisdom and understanding from God? (Job 12:12 and Proverbs 4:5-6) 38
13.	How does God compare His ways and His thoughts with the ways of the world and worldly thinking? (Isaiah 55:8-9) 39
14.	How does loving the world or the things of the world affect your love for your Father? (I John 2:15-16) 41
15.	What does the Bible say will happen if you consistently do what seems right to you from a worldly perspective? (Proverbs 14:12 and 16:25) 42
16.	What one word does the Bible use to explain what your relationship will be to God if you are a friend of the world? (James 4:4) 42

17. Why are you instructed to tremble in regard to the Word of God? Why should you be in absolute awe of the Word of God? (Isaiah 66:2 and Psalm 119:161) 43

18. What does the Bible say about the supernatural power of the Word of God? (Hebrews 4:12) 43

19. Why should older people understand the vital importance of being humble? What does God say that He will do to people who consistently are proud? (I Peter 5:5) 44

20. How will God react if you study His Word eagerly and if you work diligently at your daily Bible study? (II Timothy 2:15) 44

21. What does God instruct you to focus on instead of focusing on your external appearance? (I Samuel 16:7) 45

22. How can you be certain that the Bible was not written solely by the human authors of the Bible? (II Timothy 3:16 and I Thessalonians 2:13) 47-48

23. What results will you receive on earth and throughout eternity if you faithfully obey God's instructions to study His Word each day and to meditate day and night on the holy Scriptures? (Psalm 119:96 and II John 1:2) 48

24. Can you receive supernatural strength if you consistently study and meditate on the Word of God? (II Corinthians 4:7) 49

25. What provision has God made that will enable you to escape from the moral decay that pervades the world today? (II Peter 1:4) 49

26. How do you build yourself up spiritually to receive the glorious inheritance that Jesus Christ won for you when He rose from the dead? (Acts 20:32) 50

27. What are you instructed to do so that you will constantly be transfigured into the image of God?

(II Corinthians 3:18) 50

28. How can the power of the Word of God living in your heart help you to overcome difficult problems in your life? (Jeremiah 23:29) 51

29. What does God promise if you speak His Word continually, meditate day and night on His Word and do everything that His Word instructs you to do? (Joshua 1:8) 53

30. What does the Bible mean when it says you will be like a tree planted next to a stream of water that will never experience faded or withered leaves? If you habitually meditate day and night on the Word of God, what does God promise to you? (Psalm 1:2-3) 54-55

31. What does the Bible say about the relationship between your ears and the Word of God? (Psalm 78:1, Ezekiel 3:10 and John 8:47) 56

32. What relationship exists between your ears consistently hearing God's Word and your understanding of the Word of God? (Matthew 11:15) 56

33. What blessings will you receive if you consistently hear the Word of God and if you consistently obey God's instructions? (Isaiah 55:3 and Luke 11:28) 57

34. How does your faith in God increase? How does this spiritual truth relate to meditating day and night on the Word of God? (Romans 10:17) 57

35. Where does the Bible say that you can receive supernatural strength to meet your every need? (Philippians 4:13) 61

36. Why should you consistently store up the Word of God in your mind and your heart? (Deuteronomy 11:18 and Proverbs 7:1) 67

37. What is the spiritual foundation for your faith in God?

What are you instructed to do with the Word of God so that you will be built up spiritually? (Romans 10:8 and Job 22:23) 68

38. Where does the Bible say that the home of the Word of God should be? (Colossians 3:16) 68

39. The Word of God is Truth. How can you be certain that Satan is the father of every lie? What will happen if you consistently fill your mind and your heart with the Word of God? (John 17:17, John 8:44 and John 8:32) 69

40. What are you instructed to do to walk in victory over Satan? (I John 2:14) 69

41. Instead of focusing on bad news or anything else that Satan wants you to focus on, what does God instruct you to do? (Psalm 112:6-8) 70

42. What relationship exists between what you deeply believe in your heart and filling your heart with the Word of God? What relationship exists between what you truly believe in your heart and the words that flow out of your mouth when you face a crisis? (Proverbs 23:7 and Matthew 12:34-35) 70-71

43. What will happen to you if you have a glad heart? What will happen to you if you consistently allow sorrow to enter into your heart? (Proverbs 15:13) 71

44. Instead of allowing anxious thoughts to fill your mind and your heart, the Bible instructs you to have a glad heart. What blessings will you receive if you consistently have a glad heart? (Proverbs 15:15 and I Thessalonians 5:16) 71

45. What relationship exists between a happy heart, a cheerful mind, a broken spirit, and your health? (Proverbs 17:22) 73

46. The Bible is God's spiritual medicine. How do you partake of this spiritual medicine to receive physical healing? (Psalm 107:20 and Psalm 19:7) 73

47. The Bible is a spiritual seed. What spiritual soil has God provided where you can plant the supernatural seed of His Word? (Luke 8:11) 74

48. How does the Bible compare the importance of feeding nutritious food to your body and feeding yourself with supernatural spiritual food from the Word of God? (Job 23:12) 75

49. If you consistently eat the spiritual food that God has provided for you, what will happen to your heart? (Jeremiah 15:16) 75

50. The Bible is spiritual nourishment that your Father has provided for you. How often should you nourish yourself with the Word of God? (Matthew 4:4 and I Timothy 4:6) 75

51. What will happen if you consistently allow worry and fear to enter into your heart? What will happen if you consistently encourage your heart with the Word of God? (Proverbs 12:25) 76

52. What did God provide through the human authors of the Bible many years ago to help you in your life today? (Romans 15:4) 76

53. When the psalmist David faced severe problems, he asked God to strengthen him with His Word. What did God do in response to David's prayer? How does this principle apply to your life today? (Psalm 119:28 and Psalm 119:50) 76-77

54. What did King Jehoshaphat do when he faced an army that was much stronger than his army? How does this principle apply to your life when you face adversity that seems to be overwhelming? (II Chronicles 20:12) 79

55. God has given you the ability to direct your thoughts. What does the Bible instruct you to do in regard to directing your thoughts? (Proverbs 23:19 and II Corinthians 10:5) 79-80

56. What does the Bible say about the seeming severity of the problems you face and God's ability to solve these problems? (Jeremiah 32:17) 80

57. What does the Bible mean when you are instructed to imprint God on your mind? (Nehemiah 4:14) 80-81

58. What does the Bible say about continually looking straight ahead and not turning to the right or to the left? (Proverbs 4:27) 81

59. What did Jesus refer to when He spoke of setting His face like a flint? How does this instruction apply to your life today? (Isaiah 50:7) 81

60. Why should you continually speak the Word of God faithfully? (Jeremiah 23:28) 81-82

61. What does God instruct you to do so that He will guard you and keep you in perfect and constant peace? (Isaiah 26:3) 82

62. How do you receive great peace from God? (Psalm 119:165) 82

63. What will happen to you if you focus continually on God and His Word? (Psalm 16:8-9) 82

64. What are you instructed to do to enter into God's rest? (Hebrews 4:10) 82-83

65. What does the Bible say about the importance of focusing on what is vital instead of focusing on anything in the world? (Philippians 1:10) 83

66. How does the Bible compare the importance of spiritual fitness and physical fitness? Why is spiritual fitness more important than physical fitness? (I Timothy 4:7-8) 83

67. What does the Bible say about the importance of steadily growing into spiritual maturity? (Hebrews 6:1) 83

68. What will happen to your spiritual knowledge if you

continue to grow spiritually? What will happen to your spiritual knowledge if you do not consistently grow and mature spiritually? (Matthew 13:12) 84

69. If Jesus Christ is your Savior, why does your life belong to Him and not to you? (II Corinthians 5:15 and I Corinthians 16:19-20) 85

70. What will happen if you consistently study and meditate on the Word of God and do what God instructs you to do? (James 1:25) 85

71. What does God promise if you continually obey His instructions and seek Him with all your heart? (Psalm 119:2) 86

72. Why are you instructed to have the Word of God in your mind, in your heart and in your mouth? (Deuteronomy 30:14) 86

73. God has promised that He will make you the head and not the tail, and that you will be above the problems you face and not beneath them. What are you instructed to do to receive this blessing from God? (Deuteronomy 28:13) 86

74. What did the psalmist do when he saw people who did not love the Word of God, receive the Word of God and obey the Word of God? (Psalm 119:136) 86-87

75. What is fear of the Lord? What does God promise if you truly fear Him and delight in His Word? (Psalm 112:1 and Psalm 25:14) 87

76. What does the Bible say about the vital importance of keeping Jesus Christ in first place in your life at all times? (Colossians 1:18 and John 3:30) 87-88

77. What does the Bible say about the relationship between humility, pride, and receiving or not receiving the grace of God? (James 3:13, Psalm 25:9 and Proverbs 3:34) ... 88

78. The Bible instructs you not to focus on the things of the world that are empty and futile. Why is this instruction especially important during the final years of your life? (I Samuel 12:20-21) 88

79. How can you be certain that God sits on His throne in heaven and at the same time lives in the hearts of every one of His children on earth? (Ephesians 4:6) 91

80. How can you be certain that Jesus Christ sits next to God in heaven and also lives in the heart of every person who has received Him as his or her Savior? (II Corinthians 13:5) 91-92

81. What did the apostle Paul mean when he said that he shared the crucifixion of Jesus Christ? How does this statement apply to your life today? (Galatians 2:20) 92

82. If Jesus Christ is your Savior, how can you be certain that the Holy Spirit lives in your heart? (I Corinthians 6:19) 92

83. What is the Godhead? What awareness should you have of the enormous spiritual power that you have within you if Jesus Christ is your Savior? (Colossians 2:9-10) 93

84. What did God command Joshua to do? Why did He tell Joshua that he should not be afraid? (Joshua 1:9) 93

85. What great spiritual truth can help you above all else whenever you are tempted to be afraid of a seemingly overwhelming problem? (Isaiah 41:10) 94

86. Can you be certain that God desires to help you and to fight your battles for you? (II Chronicles 32:8) 94

87. Can you be certain that your Father will never leave you or forsake you? (Hebrews 13:5) 94

88. God is not a distant far away God. He lives in your heart if Jesus Christ is your Savior. How should this great spiritual truth apply to the way that you live every day of your life? (Acts 17:27-28 and Psalm 63:8 and I

	John 2:27) 95
89.	What people on earth are far away from God? What people have been given the opportunity to consistently draw closer to God? (Ephesians 2:13) 97
90.	You will starve if you go indefinitely without food. What word does the Bible use to describe the importance of your relationship with God being greater than your need for food for your body? (Amos 5:4) 97
91.	What is the relationship between knowing God intimately and obeying His instructions? (I John 2:3) ... 98
92.	Who decides how close your relationship with God will be? (James 4:8) 98
93.	How does the Bible instruct you to overcome the temptation to be anxious and worried? How will God react if you obey this instruction? (I Peter 3:4) 98
94.	How do you become righteous before God? What blessings does this relationship give you? How do you live a righteous life? What blessings does a righteous life provide to you? (Isaiah 32:17) 98-99
95.	Is there a relationship between calmness in your mind and your heart and the health of your body? (Proverbs 14:30) 99
96.	What does God promise to do to give you the power to remain calm when you face adversity? (Psalm 94:12-13) 99
97.	What did the apostle Paul mean when he said that he learned how to be content? How can learning this lesson apply to your life today? (Philippians 4:11) 99
98.	What is the relationship between spiritual maturity and calmness within yourself? (Proverbs 17:27 and Psalm 37:7) 100
99.	Your Father instructs you to be still and to know that He is God. How does this instruction apply to your life

when you face adversity? (Psalm 46:10) 100

100. How did the apostle Paul instruct Timothy to react to every hardship he faced? How does this instruction apply to you today? (II Timothy 4:5) 100

101. Some people take tranquilizers because they are worried and anxious. What spiritual tranquilizer did God provide to strengthen you when you face adversity? (Isaiah 30:15) 101

102. When you face seemingly severe problems, why should you be certain that God knows exactly what to do with problems that may seem to you to have no solution? (II Peter 2:9 and Psalm 46:1) 103

103. What relationship exists between your faith in God and the degree of help that you will receive from God? (Matthew 8:13) 103-104

104. How does the Bible say that people betray themselves into deception by Satan and his demons? (James 1:22) 104

105. Instead of relying on the limitations of your human knowledge and understanding, what does the Word of God instruct you to do? (Proverbs 3:5-6) 104

106. How can you be absolutely certain that God stands behind every promise in His Word? (Joshua 23:14) 104

107. The Word of God is much more powerful than you can comprehend with the limitations of your human understanding. Why should you love the Word of God and obey God's instructions? (Psalm 119:129) 105

108. God knows every problem that every person on earth faces. How does He react to your trust in His Word when you face severe adversity? (Jeremiah 1:12) 107

109. What is required for your faith in God to be deep, strong and unwavering regardless of the circumstances

you face? (Colossians 1:23 and II Corinthians 5:7) 107

110. What is Mt. Zion? How is your faith in God compared to Mt. Zion? (Psalm 125:1) 107

111. What does the Bible say is absolutely necessary for you to please God? (Hebrews 11:6) 108

112. How does *The Amplified Bible* describe faith in God? Do these words describe your faith in God? (Hebrews 10:22) 108

113. How does God promise to react if you trust Him completely, commit everything to Him and absolutely refuse to be afraid? (Psalm 84:12) 108

114. What does God promise if you obey the instructions in His Word and trust completely in Him at all times regardless of the circumstances you face? (Proverbs 16:20, Romans 9:33 and Romans 10:11) 109

115. What did the psalmist David say that he was certain would happen to him if he turned to God for his strength and protection and trusted completely in God? (Psalm 28:7) 109

116. What relationship exists between the intimacy of your relationship with God and drawing supernatural strength from Him? (Ephesians 6:10) 110

117. Why is it important for your trust in God to be childlike during the final years of your life? (Luke 18:17) 110

118. What does the Bible mean when it speaks of tradition? What effect does traditional thinking have on the supernatural power of God's Word? (Matthew 15:6) 111

119. Many older people focus on the past. What does God instruct you to do in regard to focusing on the past? (Isaiah 43:18-19 and Job 11:16-18) 113

120. What one area does the Bible instruct you to focus on in regard to the past? (Job 37:14, Deuteronomy 8:2, Psalm

  77:11-12 and Psalm 145:5) 114-115

121. What does God instruct you to do about being afraid of what might happen in the future? (Revelation 2:10) ... 115

122. Will the Holy Spirit show discerning Christians what will happen in the future? (John 16:13) 116

123. What did Jesus instruct you to do in regard to worrying about what might happen in the future? (Matthew 6:34) 116

124. How does God instruct you to react to each day that He has given to you? (Psalm 118:24) 117

125. How often did Jesus tell His disciples to trust God to provide them with food? (Luke 11:3) 117

126. How frequently does God promise to strengthen you? (Deuteronomy 33:25) 118

127. How can you be certain that God wants to direct your steps? (Psalm 37:23 and Proverbs 16:9) 118

128. What is God's desire in regard to anxiety and distress in your life? (I Corinthians 7:32) 118

129. What did Jesus Christ tell you to be on guard about in regard to your heart? (Luke 21:34) 119

130. What advice does Jesus give to people who are chronic worriers? (Matthew 6:25) 119

131. Instead of allowing your heart to be troubled, what did Jesus instruct you to do? (John 14:1) 119

132. What does the Word of God instruct you to do whenever you are tempted to be anxious about anything? What result does God promise you if you do this? (Philippians 4:6-7) 119

133. What does the Bible say about basing your prayers on promises in the Word of God? (Isaiah 62:6) 120

134. How long does God promise to bear your burdens and

care for you? (Psalm 68:19) 120

135. What does the Bible say about a strong and capable man controlling his own life? (Jeremiah 10:23) 120

136. What does the Bible mean when you are instructed to cast your burden on the Lord? What does God promise to do if you do this? (Psalm 55:22) 121

137. What does God instruct you to do when you cast your cares on Him? (I Peter 5:6-7) 121

138. What does God promise to do for you if you commit your way to Him and trust Him completely? (Psalm 37:5) 121

139. What did the psalmist David say about his knowledge of God's plan for his life? (Psalm 139:16) 123

140. What relationship is there between receiving Jesus Christ as your Savior and being able to carry out God's assignment for your life? Does God have a very specific plan for your life? (Ephesians 2:10) 123

141. God gave you specific talents when He created you. What did He give you these talents for? (Romans 12:6-8) 124

142. What does the Bible say about God's instructions for retirement of Levites? What should you aspire to do when you retire? (Numbers 8:23-26) 124-125

143. What does the Bible instruct older people to do with what they have learned during their lives? (Joel 1:2-3) 125

144. What does God instruct you to do if you live for many years? (Ecclesiastes 11:8) 125

145. Can you be certain that God created you to live a long and productive life? (Job 5:26) 125

146. What does the Bible say about some of the dreams that older people have? (Acts 2:17) 125

147. What attitude did the psalmist have regarding his old age? How does this attitude apply to the final years of your life? (Psalm 71:18) 126

148. When the apostle Paul was an old man, how did he refer to himself in regard to Jesus Christ? (Philemon 1:9) 126

149. What does the Bible say about fruitfulness during your old age and your contentment and fulfillment? (Psalm 92:14) 126

150. What did Jesus explain in regard to the comparison between God's will being done on earth and God's will in heaven? (Luke 11:2) 129

151. What did Jesus say about His desire to do what He wanted to do? What was the focus of His life? (John 5:30) 129

152. What does God mean when He promises to progressively reveal His will for your life? (Acts 22:14) 130

153. God lives in the heart of every person who has received Jesus Christ as his or her Savior. What does God Who lives in your heart promise to do in regard to helping you to carry out His assignment for your life? (Philippians 2:13) 130

154. What did the apostle Paul say about the severe adversity he faced during his life and his commitment to complete the assignment that Jesus gave to him? (Acts 20:24) 131

155. What advice did the apostle Paul give to the church in Macedonia about completing God's plan for each person's life? How does this instruction apply to your commitment to seek, find and carry out God's will for your life? (II Corinthians 8:5) 131

156. What did the psalmist say that he was committed to do before he died? (Psalm 118:17) 131

157. What does the Bible say about the degree of commitment you should have to carry out God's will for your life? (I Corinthians 15:58 and Romans 12:11) 131-132

158. What will happen if you consistently pray earnestly from your heart? (James 5:16) 132

159. What instructions did Jesus Christ give about persevering when you pray? What will God do if you consistently persevere in your prayers of faith?
(Luke 11:9-10) 132

160. Why should you consistently seek more details about God's will for your life? (Colossians 1:9) 133

161. What does the Bible instruct you to do to make the very most of the final years of your life? (Ephesians 5:15-17 and II Timothy 2:22) 135

162. Instead of focusing on personal goals, what does God's Word instruct you to focus on? (Proverbs 19:21) 135-136

163. What relationship exists between consistently renewing your mind by studying God's Word and finding and carrying out God's perfect will for your life? (Romans 12:2) 136

164. What does God promise to be if you fervently pursue His will for your life? Can you be assured that everything that happens while you are pursuing God's will for your life will work out for the best?
(Romans 8:28) 136-137

165. Can human beings find lasting satisfaction and fulfillment from the pursuit of worldly goals? (Ecclesiastes 1:8) 137

166. When God created you, what did He place in your heart and your mind that can only be satisfied by Him? (Ecclesiastes 3:11) 137

167. What does God promise if you hunger to complete His assignment for your life? (Psalm 107:9) 137

168. What will God say to you in heaven if you successfully complete His assignment for your life on earth? (Matthew 25:21) 137-138

169. Why should older people be very careful not to fall into the habit of watching television indiscriminately? (Mark 4:24) 140

170. What does it mean to fear the Lord? What relationship is there between truly fearing the Lord and your physical health? (Proverbs 3:7-8) 146

171. What does the Bible mean when you are instructed to continually keep the Word of God at the forefront of your consciousness? Why are you instructed to guard what comes into your heart diligently? (Proverbs 4:20-23) 146

172. What did the prophet Isaiah prophesy that Jesus Christ would do to provide healing for you? What does the New Testament say about the fulfillment of this prophecy in the Old Testament? (Isaiah 53:4-5 and I Peter 2:24) 147

173. What relationship exists between the words that you constantly speak when you are sick and receiving healing from God? (Proverbs 12:18, Proverbs 16:24 and Matthew 12:34-35) 148-149

174. Jesus, Paul and other Christians walked many miles as part of their normal everyday lives. What does the Bible say about the long distances that Jesus and Paul walked? (Matthew 15:21 and Acts 20:13) 154

175. What did the apostle Paul say about his commitment to be in good physical condition by disciplining his body? (I Corinthians 9:26-27) 159

176. Perspiration from exercise can be very important to good health. What does the Bible say about the perspiration that people working in the fields in Bible times experienced? (Genesis 3:19) 162

177. Why should you be determined to consistently cleanse both your body and your spirit? (II Corinthians 7:1) ... 162

178. Will God give you supernatural energy if you are completely devoted to completing His assignment for your life? (Colossians 1:29) 172

179. There is a direct relationship between physical energy and adequate sleep. What did God promise in regard to your sleep? (Psalm 127:2 and Proverbs 3:24) 172

180. How important is your death to God? (Psalm 116:15) 179

181. What does the Bible refer to when it speaks of walking through the valley of the shadow of death? What does God promise to do when you go through this valley? (Psalm 23:4) 179

182. Satan and his demons want you to be afraid of death. What price did Jesus Christ pay to deliver you from the fear of death? (Hebrews 2:14-15 and Revelation 1:17-18) 179-180

183. What did the prophet Isaiah prophesy about the victory that Jesus Christ would win over death? What does the New Testament say about the fulfillment of this Old Testament prophecy? (Isaiah 25:8 and I Corinthians 15:54-55) 180-181

184. What does the Bible mean when it says that Jesus Christ annulled death? (II Timothy 1:10) 181

185. What does the Bible say about the positive aspects of the death of a Christian? (Proverbs 14:32 and Philippians 1:21) 181-182

186. Unbelievers look at death as the end. Why should Christians look at death as a glorious beginning? (John 14:19) 182

187. What is required for your name to be enrolled as a citizen of heaven? (I Peter 1:4 and Luke 10:20) 183

188. If Jesus Christ is your Savior, where is your real home? What does the Bible instruct you to focus on? (Philippians 3:20, II Corinthians 4:18 and Colossians 3:2-3) 183-184

189. Can you even remotely comprehend the glory of heaven with the limitations of your human understanding? (I Corinthians 2:9) 184

190. Why is there never any darkness in heaven? Where does light come from in heaven? (Revelation 22:5) 185

192. Why will your heart constantly sing with joy when you are in heaven? (Isaiah 35:10) 185

193. If Jesus Christ is your Savior, can you be certain that you will see Him face to face? (I John 3:2 and Isaiah 33:17) 185-186

194. You should focus on completing God's assignment for your life on earth. However, why should you also focus on the magnificence of heaven? (Philippians 1:23 and I Thessalonians 4:17-18) 186

195. How can Jesus continually have intimate conversations with every person in heaven at the same time? (Ephesians 4:6) 186-187

196. Why will there be no sorrow, grief or pain in heaven? (Revelation 21:4) 189

197. What does the Bible say about the difference between your earthly body and your heavenly body? (I Corinthians 15:40, I Corinthians 15:42-43 and II Corinthians 5:1) 189-190

198. Why is your earthly body described by the Bible as being a tent? How will the condition of your heavenly body compare with the physical condition of your earthly body? (II Corinthians 5:2) 180

199. What does the Bible mean when it says that the spirits of the righteous will be made perfect in heaven? How

does this scriptural truth apply to the relationship that all people in heaven will have with other inhabitants of heaven? (Hebrews 12:23 and Revelation 22:3) 191

200. Will you remember the problems that you had on earth when you are in heaven? (Isaiah 65:17) 191

201. Will you see God face to face when you are in heaven? Will God give you the complete understanding that you did not have during your life on earth? (I Corinthians 13:12) 192-193

202. Will you be rewarded in heaven for successfully completing the assignment that God gave you to complete during your life on earth? (Ephesians 6:8 and Revelation 14:13) 193

203. If you were persecuted for your Christian beliefs during your life on earth, what will God do for you in heaven as a result of the persecution you went through on earth? (Matthew 5:11-12) 194

A Few Words About Lamplight Ministries

Lamplight Ministries, Inc. originally began in 1983 as Lamplight Publications. After ten years as a publishing firm with a goal of selling Christian books, Lamplight Ministries was founded in 1993. Jack and Judy Hartman founded Lamplight Ministries with a mission of continuing to sell their publications and also to *give* large numbers of these publications free of charge to needy people all over the world.

Lamplight Ministries was created to allow people who have been blessed by our publications to share in financing the translation, printing and distribution of our books into other languages and also to distribute our publications free of charge to inmates in jails and prisons. Over the years many partners of Lamplight Ministries have shared Jack and Judy's vision. As the years have gone by Lamplight Ministries' giving has increased with each passing year. Thousands of people in jails and prisons and in Third World countries have received our publications free of charge.

Our books and Scripture Meditation Cards have been translated into eleven foreign languages – Armenian, Danish, Greek, Hebrew, German, Korean, Norwegian, Portuguese, Russian, Spanish and the Tamil dialect in India. The translations in these languages are not available from Lamplight Ministries in the United States. These translations can only be obtained in the countries where they have been printed.

The pastors of many churches in Third World countries have written to say that they consistently preach sermons in their churches based on the scriptural contents of our publications. We believe that people in several churches in many different countries consistently hear sermons that are based on the scriptural contents of our publications. Praise the Lord!

Jack Hartman was the sole author of twelve Christian books. After co-authoring one book with Judy, Jack and Judy co-authored ten sets of Scripture Meditation Cards. Judy has been the co-author of every subsequent book. Jack and Judy currently are working on other books that they believe the Lord is leading them to write as co-authors.

We invite you to request our newsletters to stay in touch with us, to learn of our latest publications and to read comments from people all over the world. Please write, fax, call or email us. You are very special to us. We love you and thank God for you. Our heart is to take the gospel to the world and for our books to be available in every known language. Hallelujah!

Lamplight Ministries, Inc.,

PO Box 1307 - Dunedin, Florida, 34697. USA

Phone: 1-800-540-1597 • Fax: 1-727-784-2980

website: lamplight.net • email: lamplight@lamplight.net

We offer you a substantial quantity discount

From the beginning of our ministry we have been led of the Lord to offer the same quantity discount to individuals that we offer to Christian bookstores. Each individual has a sphere of influence with a specific group of people. We believe that you know many people who need to learn the scriptural contents of our publications.

The Word of God encourages us to give freely to others. We encourage you to give selected copies of these publications to people you know who need help in the specific areas that are covered by our publications. See our order form for specific information on the quantity discounts that we make available to you so that you can share our books, Scripture Meditation Cards and CDs with others.

A request to our readers

If this book has helped you, we would like to receive your comments so that we can share them with others. Your comments can encourage other people to study our publications to learn from the scriptural contents of these publications.

When we receive a letter containing comments on any of our books, cassette tapes or Scripture Meditation Cards, we prayerfully take out excerpts from these letters. These selected excerpts are included in our newsletters and occasionally in our advertising and promotional materials.

If any of our publications have been a blessing to you, please share your comments with us so that we can share them with others. Tell us in your own words what a specific publication has meant to you and why you would recommend it to others. Please give as much specific information as possible. We prefer three or four paragraphs so that we can condense this into one paragraph.

Thank you for taking a few minutes of your time to encourage other people to learn from the scripture references in our publications.

ORDER FORM FOR BOOKS

Book Title	Quantity	Total
What Does God Say? ($18)	_____ x $18 =	_____
Effective Prayer ($14)	_____ x $14 =	_____
God's Instructions for Growing Older ($14)	_____ x $14 =	_____
A Close and Intimate Relationship with God ($14)	_____ x $14 =	_____
God's Joy Regardless of Circumstances ($14)	_____ x $14 =	_____
Victory Over Adversity ($14)	_____ x $14 =	_____
Receive Healing from the Lord ($14)	_____ x $14 =	_____
Unshakable Faith in Almighty God ($14)	_____ x $14 =	_____
Exchange Your Worries for God's Perfect Peace ($14)	_____ x $14 =	_____
God's Wisdom is Available to You ($14)	_____ x $14 =	_____
Overcoming Fear ($14)	_____ x $14 =	_____
Trust God For Your Finances ($10)	_____ x $10 =	_____
What Will Heaven Be Like? ($10)	_____ x $10 =	_____
Quiet Confidence in the Lord ($10)	_____ x $10 =	_____
Never, Never Give Up ($10)	_____ x $10 =	_____
Increased Energy and Vitality ($10)	_____ x $10 =	_____
God's Will for Our Lives ($10)	_____ x $10 =	_____
How to Study the Bible ($7)	_____ x $7 =	_____
Nuggets of Faith ($7)	_____ x $7 =	_____
100 Years From Today ($7)	_____ x $7 =	_____

Price of books _____

    Minus 40% discount for 5-9 books _____

    Minus 50% discount for 10 or more books _____

    Net price of order _____

    Add 15% **before discount** for shipping and handling _____

    Florida residents only, add 7% sales tax _____

    Tax deductible contribution to Lamplight Ministries, Inc. _____

Enclosed check or money order (do not send cash) _____
(Foreign orders must be submitted in U.S. dollars.)

Please make check payable to **Lamplight Ministries, Inc.** and mail to:
PO Box 1307, Dunedin, FL 34697

MC____ Visa____ AmEx____ Disc.____ Card #_____

Exp Date _____ Signature _____

Name _____

Address _____

City _____

State or Province _____ Zip or Postal Code _____

ORDER FORM FOR BOOKS

Book Title	Quantity	Total
What Does God Say? ($18)	_____x $18 =	_____
Effective Prayer ($14)	_____x $14 =	_____
God's Instructions for Growing Older ($14)	_____x $14 =	_____
A Close and Intimate Relationship with God ($14)	_____x $14 =	_____
God's Joy Regardless of Circumstances ($14)	_____x $14 =	_____
Victory Over Adversity ($14)	_____x $14 =	_____
Receive Healing from the Lord ($14)	_____x $14 =	_____
Unshakable Faith in Almighty God ($14)	_____x $14 =	_____
Exchange Your Worries for God's Perfect Peace ($14)	_____x $14 =	_____
God's Wisdom is Available to You ($14)	_____x $14 =	_____
Overcoming Fear ($14)	_____x $14 =	_____
Trust God For Your Finances ($10)	_____x $10 =	_____
What Will Heaven Be Like? ($10)	_____x $10 =	_____
Quiet Confidence in the Lord ($10)	_____x $10 =	_____
Never, Never Give Up ($10)	_____x $10 =	_____
Increased Energy and Vitality ($10)	_____x $10 =	_____
God's Will for Our Lives ($10)	_____x $10 =	_____
How to Study the Bible ($7)	_____x $7 =	_____
Nuggets of Faith ($7)	_____x $7 =	_____
100 Years From Today ($7)	_____x $7 =	_____

Price of books _____

    Minus 40% discount for 5-9 books _____

    Minus 50% discount for 10 or more books _____

    Net price of order _____

    Add 15% **before discount** for shipping and handling _____

    Florida residents only, add 7% sales tax _____

    Tax deductible contribution to Lamplight Ministries, Inc. _____

Enclosed check or money order (do not send cash) _____
(Foreign orders must be submitted in U.S. dollars.)

Please make check payable to **Lamplight Ministries, Inc.** and mail to:
PO Box 1307, Dunedin, FL 34697

MC____ Visa____ AmEx____ Disc.____ Card # _____

Exp Date _____ Signature _____

Name _____

Address _____

City _____

State or Province _____ Zip or Postal Code _____

ORDER FORM FOR SCRIPTURE MEDITATION CARDS AND CDs

SCRIPTURE MEDITATION CARDS	QUANTITY	PRICE
Find God's Will for Your Life ($5)	_____	_____
Financial Instructions from God ($5)	_____	_____
Freedom from Worry and Fear ($5)	_____	_____
A Closer Relationship with the Lord ($5)	_____	_____
Our Father's Wonderful Love ($5)	_____	_____
Receive Healing from the Lord ($5)	_____	_____
Receive God's Blessing in Adversity ($5)	_____	_____
Enjoy God's Wonderful Peace ($5)	_____	_____
God is Always with You ($5)	_____	_____
Continually Increasing Faith in God ($5)	_____	_____

CDs	QUANTITY	PRICE
Find God's Will for Your Life ($10)	_____	_____
Financial Instructions from God ($10)	_____	_____
Freedom from Worry and Fear ($10)	_____	_____
A Closer Relationship with the Lord ($10)	_____	_____
Our Father's Wonderful Love ($10)	_____	_____
Receive Healing from the Lord ($10)	_____	_____
Receive God's Blessing in Adversity ($10)	_____	_____
Enjoy God's Wonderful Peace ($10)	_____	_____
God is Always with You ($10)	_____	_____
Continually Increasing Faith in God ($10)	_____	_____

TOTAL PRICE _____

Minus 40% discount for 5-9 Scripture Cards and CDs _____
Minus 50% discount for 10 or more Scripture Cards and CDs _____
Net price of order _____
Add 15% **before discount** for shipping and handling _____
Florida residents only, add 7% sales tax _____
Tax deductible contribution to Lamplight Ministries, Inc. _____
Enclosed check or money order (do not send cash) _____
(Foreign orders must be submitted in U.S. dollars.)

Please make check payable to **Lamplight Ministries, Inc.** and mail to:
PO Box 1307, Dunedin, FL 34697

MC____ Visa____ AmEx____ Disc.____ Card # _____

Exp Date _____ Signature _____

Name _____

Address _____

City _____

State or Province _____ Zip or Postal Code _____

ORDER FORM FOR SCRIPTURE MEDITATION CARDS AND CDs

SCRIPTURE MEDITATION CARDS	QUANTITY	PRICE
Find God's Will for Your Life ($5)	_____	_____
Financial Instructions from God ($5)	_____	_____
Freedom from Worry and Fear ($5)	_____	_____
A Closer Relationship with the Lord ($5)	_____	_____
Our Father's Wonderful Love ($5)	_____	_____
Receive Healing from the Lord ($5)	_____	_____
Receive God's Blessing in Adversity ($5)	_____	_____
Enjoy God's Wonderful Peace ($5)	_____	_____
God is Always with You ($5)	_____	_____
Continually Increasing Faith in God ($5)	_____	_____

CDs	QUANTITY	PRICE
Find God's Will for Your Life ($10)	_____	_____
Financial Instructions from God ($10)	_____	_____
Freedom from Worry and Fear ($10)	_____	_____
A Closer Relationship with the Lord ($10)	_____	_____
Our Father's Wonderful Love ($10)	_____	_____
Receive Healing from the Lord ($10)	_____	_____
Receive God's Blessing in Adversity ($10)	_____	_____
Enjoy God's Wonderful Peace ($10)	_____	_____
God is Always with You ($10)	_____	_____
Continually Increasing Faith in God ($10)	_____	_____

TOTAL PRICE _____

Minus 40% discount for 5-9 Scripture Cards and CDs _____
Minus 50% discount for 10 or more Scripture Cards and CDs _____
Net price of order _____
Add 15% ***before discount*** for shipping and handling _____
Florida residents only, add 7% sales tax _____
Tax deductible contribution to Lamplight Ministries, Inc. _____
Enclosed check or money order (do not send cash) _____
(Foreign orders must be submitted in U.S. dollars.)

Please make check payable to **Lamplight Ministries, Inc.** and mail to:
PO Box 1307, Dunedin, FL 34697

MC____ Visa____ AmEx____ Disc.____ Card #_____

Exp Date _____ Signature _____

Name _____

Address _____

City _____

State or Province _____ Zip or Postal Code _____

www.ingramcontent.com/pod-product-compliance
Lightning Source LLC
Chambersburg PA
CBHW071524040426
42452CB00008B/883